VICTORIAN FLOWER GARDENS

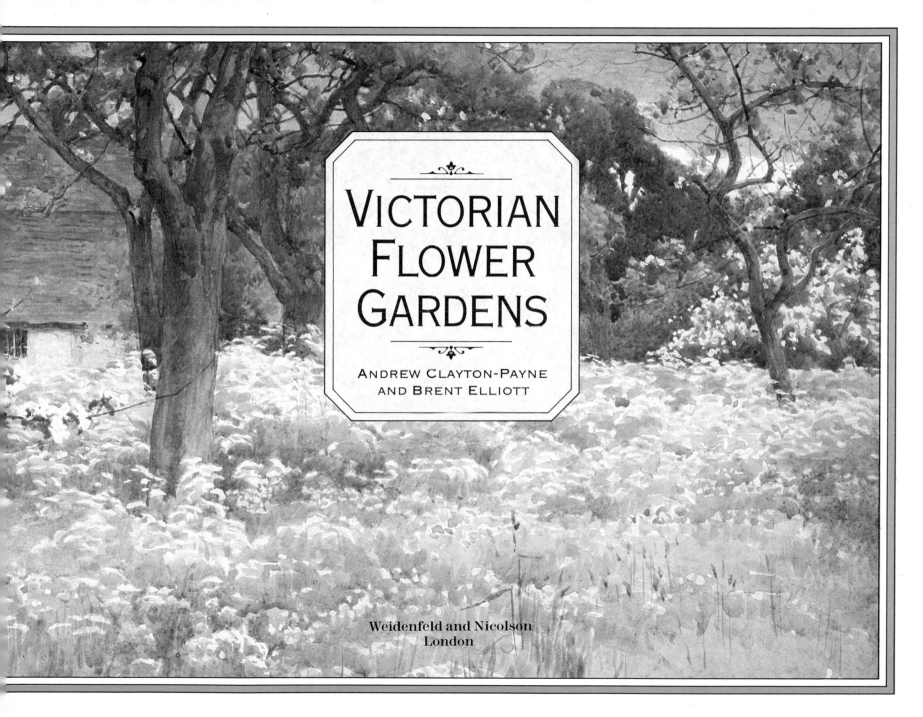

VICTORIAN FLOWER GARDENS

ANDREW CLAYTON-PAYNE
AND BRENT ELLIOTT

Weidenfeld and Nicolson
London

For Ghalia

© Text George Weidenfeld and Nicolson Ltd 1988

First published in 1988 by George Weidenfeld and Nicolson Ltd
91 Clapham High Street, London SW4 7TA

Design Styling by Bernard Higton
Designer: Ruth Hope

British Library Cataloguing in Publication Data

Clayton-Payne, Andrew
 Victorian flower gardens
 1. English paintings, 1837–1901. Special
 subjects. Gardens. Flowering plants
 I. Title   II. Elliott, Brent
 758′.5

ISBN 0–297–79443–4 cased

Front cover: FEEDING THE CHICKENS, *Arthur Claude Strachan*
Back cover: A SUMMER'S WALK, *Helen Allingham*
Half-title: GIRL ON A HAMMOCK, *Edward Killingworth Johnson*
Title: MRS BODENHAM'S ORCHARD, HEREFORD, *Alfred Parsons*
Contents: THE NOSEGAY, CHELSEA, *Rose Barton*

Phototypeset by Keyspools Ltd, Golborne, Lancs
Colour separations by Newsele Litho Ltd
Printed in Italy by Printers Srl, Trento
Bound by L.E.G.O., Vicenza

CONTENTS

AUTHORS' ACKNOWLEDGEMENTS

I would like to thank everyone who has been so generous with their invaluable help. In particular, I am greatly indebted to Sarah Colgrave of Sotheby's, Mr & Mrs L. Guthrie of Fine-Lines Fine Art, Ric James of the Priory Gallery, Diana Kay of Phillips, Claudia Brigg of Christie's, Eric Ford of the Kenulf Gallery, Chris Beetles, Sheila Hinde, David James, John Thompson, Richard Hagen, the Leger Galleries, the Christopher Wood Gallery, the Heim Gallery and the many private collectors who so kindly agreed to allow their beautiful pictures to be reproduced. I am also very much indebted to Emma Way of Weidenfeld and Nicolson who, with great adroitness, has handled the project from beginning to end. Finally, I would like to thank my wife for her unflagging support and enthusiasm since the inception of the idea for the book.

Andrew Clayton-Payne

I should also like to thank my wife for coping with me during my share of the work on this book. Grateful thanks are also due to Sally Kington.

Brent Elliott

INTRODUCTION

hat, asked the Leeds-based landscape gardener Joshua Major at the beginning of the Victorian period, 'has the painter to do with the gay parterre, the delightful flower garden, – the soul's delight of the majority of mankind?' The question at first appears incongruous: after all, the present book is devoted to paintings of nineteenth-century flower gardens, many of them by artists who took the garden as the special theme of their careers. Yet Major's question should alert us to an important fact: the overwhelming majority of these paintings date from the latter part of Victoria's reign, and from the brief reign that followed. The developments in gardening that took place between the 1820s and 1850s – possibly the most exciting and innovative period in garden history – went largely unrecorded by contemporary painters, who were drawn instead to the landscape as their theme.

The reasons for this neglect of the garden in early Victorian painting are not hard to find. For roughly a century before Victoria's accession, the English garden had been identified, not with the flower garden, but with the landscape. The eighteenth century sought to make a continuity between the garden and the broader landscape, which was thought of in terms of an idealized 'nature'; as little as possible in the view from the country house windows was to tell of the hand of man. Undulating landform, clumps and belts of trees – serpentine water – these constituted the important part of the garden. The illusion of continuity was provided by the ha-ha, or sunk fence, a handy device for keeping cattle at a distance without any obvious visual barrier. This was the accustomed subject of the landscape painter.

The portrayal of gardens had become an established practice by the early eighteenth century, before the landscape style had arisen, at a time when large English gardens tended to consist of a series of differentiated areas, demarcated from each other by hedges and walls. The characteristic garden picture of this period, whether in the engravings of Kip and Knyff or in the work of a native school of rather naïve painters, shows a perspec-

THE ORCHARD
Helen Allingham

tive or bird's-eye view of compartment after compartment spreading out across the land. The most accomplished garden pictures of the time are to be found in the work of artists such as Pieter Andreas Rysbrack (see his views of Chiswick, commissioned by the 3rd Earl of Burlington about 1730) or Balthasar Nebot (see his views of Hartwell House a decade later). The rigid formalized lines of sculpted hedges and carefully spaced trees lent themselves well to an almost geometric style of composition.

In the second half of the century, however, such geometry was rejected in favour of an open, asymmetrical composition suited to the 'natural' landscapes that were being created from the 1740s. From William Marlow's views of Castle Howard in the 1770s, to Turner's views of Petworth in the early nineteenth century, a flourishing school of painting promoted the image of the landscape garden. The portrayal of a garden was moving progressively closer to the depiction of a wild scene. By the end of the eighteenth century the word 'picturesque' had been coined to describe this sort of landscape – the sort worthy of being painted.

In all these cases, the artists were portraying gardens that had been designed within the preceding twenty years or so; their work recorded garden design rather than influencing it.

There was certainly a place for flowers in the eighteenth century garden, but on the country estate at least they were not to form part of the main view; flower beds were too obviously artificial to form part of the 'natural' landscape, but they could be segregated into a space enclosed by shrubberies or plantations. The best-known of such gardens in the late eighteenth century was that created by the poet William Mason at Nuneham, the subject of some well-known watercolours by Paul Sandby (though Sandby's views were an exception to the general rule). The theorists of the picturesque explicitly excluded flowers as unsuitable for painting. The foreground of a landscape painting ought to be dark, the colours becoming progressively lighter as they faded into the distance; even the spring blossom of trees was 'too distinct and splendid', according to Uvedale Price, and would destroy the unity of a painting.

This was the sort of painting that the gardeners of the early Victorian period were familiar with, and they strove to distance themselves from it. Paintings could give them no help with the floral effects they wanted to achieve; why should they acknowledge them as a standard? The landscape painter and the gardener, accordingly, spent between a quarter and half a century condemning each other as irrelevant to their respective arts. During these years, however, a revolution took place in painting: a freedom to depict local colour accurately, without having to make it conform to the dictates of an overall scheme. It was after this revolution, begun by Turner and Constable, and made more general by Mulready, the watercolourists, and the Pre-Raphaelites, that painters began to find in the bright and anti-'picturesque' colours of the flower garden a fitting subject. Consequently, most of these paintings date from the last quarter of the nineteenth century, and the first decade or so of the twentieth.

The development of flower-garden painting began in the 1860s with the work of Frederick Walker and Birket Foster, still basically under the influence of picturesque values, both in choice of subject and in the control of colours. Walker, whose early death was regarded as a tragedy for English art, was strongly influenced by the colour and technique of the Pre-Raphaelites, and the few garden scenes that he produced in the late 1860s were much admired. The Pre-Raphaelite influence is most evident in his palette and in his minute and detailed representation of natural objects, but his work never allowed such detail to obscure the human interest of the character portrayed. 'An Amateur' (see p.79), which depicts a coachman in a kitchen garden cutting a cabbage, is representative of his work.

Walker's integration of figures with their environment had a great impact on Myles Birket Foster, the artist whose name is most closely associated with Victorian watercolours. Birket Foster seldom painted gardens for their own sake, but his cottage scenes frequently included some detail of the accompanying gardens, and the popularity of these paintings ensured that views of cottage gardens became common a decade before those of grander gardens. The work of Birket Foster still essentially obeyed the dictates of picturesque colour control – an avoidance of bright flower colours that would conflict with the overall tone of the paintings – as can be seen if his paintings in this volume are compared with those of, say, Strachan or Woodlock; but through his work and that of Walker the depiction of flower gardens established itself as a genre.

The next figure to emerge was Helen Allingham, whose cottage garden scenes rivalled Birket Foster's in popularity and, thanks to new techniques in printing methods, were reproduced in such books as *Happy England* and *The Homes and Haunts of Tennyson*. She and Birket Foster both lived in the village of Witley, in Surrey, and a school of cottage garden painters grew up around them, feeding an enormous market for paintings of such subjects.

In the late nineteenth century, interest in art became more widespread as a result of numerous societies and commercial galleries holding regular exhibitions, often devoted to one artist, such as the Dowdeswell Gallery which in 1904 held an exhibition of garden pictures by Beatrice Parsons. George Elgood was to hold more than a dozen one-man shows at the Fine Art Society in New Bond Street. One outcome of this was the interest in and

HATFIELD HOUSE, HERTFORDSHIRE
L. N. Nottage

patronage of garden painters – such as the Stannards – by the royal family.

By the late 1880s, the gardens of the great were joining those of the poor in exhibitions and galleries, and the colours used in depicting their flowers were becoming progressively brighter. As this trend grew, so two different approaches became distinguishable. One was the manner associated with the names of George Samuel Elgood and Ernest Arthur Rowe, and reflected a nostalgia for old-fashioned gardens with statues, sundials, and sculpted hedges silhouetted against the sky. Rowe's pictures tend to be more rigidly organized than Elgood's, and many have almost mathematically structured compositions; his methodical approach to composition harks back to the work of garden painters of the pre-landscape period, but with the novel freedom of late nineteenth-century colour values. Elgood, similarly, used a symphony of varied colours to suggest the array of different flowers, and to offset the subtle greens of hedges and lawns. At the opposite extreme from the strong line and precise detail of their paintings were the quasi-impressionist pictures of painters like Mildred Anne Butler or, even more emphatically, David Woodlock, who worked in the early part of this century and was influenced by the colour experiments of his post-impressionist contemporaries on the Continent. He was not interested in carefully delineating individual flowers, wanting instead to recreate the visual impact of

a mass of different blooms of all shapes and sizes; the success of his technique lay in his application of watercolour to wet paper, running carefully chosen colours together to create the desired effect.

The conflict between the gardener and the painter, so apparent in the early Victorian period, had ended. By this time, however, standards of taste in gardening were changing, and much of early Victorian gardening faced increasing condemnation. The reader will find here little of the high contrast of colour which was such a feature of the flower garden until the 1870s; nothing of the brilliance and extravagance of gardens like Chatsworth and Elvaston Castle; nothing of the more elaborate forms of mid-century bedding like geranium pyramids and floral baskets. By the 1880s, the proponents of a new taste in gardening were pointing to the lack of paintings of early and high Victorian gardening as evidence of its bad taste: 'Artists of real power would paint gardens and home landscapes if there were real pictures to draw', wrote William Robinson, 'but generally they are so rare that the work does not come into the artist's view at all.' As his and similar voices urged the gardener to 'follow the true artist', the painter of gardens was thrust into the role of a model of taste. Paintings such as those reproduced in this volume are not merely a record of what the painter saw; their selection of subjects played a positive role in shaping the gardening world at the end of the nineteenth century.

IN THE ORCHARD
Myles Birket Foster

THE COTTAGE GARDEN OBSERVED

 Y the last quarter of the nineteenth century, the cottage garden was emerging as a popular theme in painting; by the beginning of the twentieth, it could make the fortune of an aspiring artist. But when one compares the cottage gardens shown in the paintings of Birket Foster in the 1860s and 1870s with, say, a Strachan or a Woodlock cottage garden in the Edwardian period, one cannot but be struck by the transformation. Vegetable plots and the signs of poverty have been replaced by billowing masses of bright flowers. Does this reflect a genuine transformation in the cottage garden, or merely the creation of a popular image?

The rustic cottage was already a popular subject for artists to sketch by the beginning of the nineteenth century, and such proponents of the picturesque as Uvedale Price recommended the building of cottages in order to provide suitable views. James Malton's *Essay on British Cottage Architecture* (1798) gave specific instructions on the design of cottages so as to provide the best contrasts of, among other things, light and shade. But the taste that designed buildings for the spectator's pleasure rather than the convenience of the inhabitants came under fire during the Victorian period; Loudon, Ruskin, Dickens, and other reformers fulminated against the taste that condemned people to live in squalor for the sake of the picture they made. Their complaints were summed up by Tom Taylor in his poem on 'Old Cottages':

> The cottage-homes of England! Yes, I know,
> How picturesque their moss and weather-stain,
> Their golden thatch, whose squared eves shadows
>   throw
> On white-washed wall and deep-sunk latticed pane...
> The kindly nature that still masks decay
> With flowers, and hues only less fair than flowers,
> All these I know, – know, too, the plagues that prey
> On those who dwell in these bepainted bowers:
> The foul miasma of their crowded rooms,
> Unaired, unlit, with green damps moulded o'er,
> The fever that each autumn deals its dooms
> From the rank ditch that stagnates by the door;
> And then I wish the picturesqueness less,
> And welcome the utilitarian hand
> That from such foulness plucks its masquing dress,
> And bids the well-aired, well-drained cottage stand,
> All bare of weather-stain, right-angled true,
> By sketches shunned, but shunned by fevers too.

Taylor's poem was one of several written to accompany a series of engravings published in 1863 as *Birket Foster's Pictures of English Landscape*. There is a considerable irony in this fact, for Birket Foster, despite being thus allied with the cause of reform, helped to perpetuate the picturesque image of the cottage through his pictures; when Tennyson asked him why he always chose tumbledown cottages to paint, he replied that 'no one likes an unbroken line'.

Birket Foster's are, nonetheless, the most realistic and least sentimental of any of the images of labourers' cottages and their gardens that we shall see – most tellingly so in their representation of children. Birket Foster's children, and to a lesser extent those of Helen Allingham, are often glimpsed working – carrying food or firewood most commonly – or accompanying and watching their elders work. The 1833 Factory Act had abolished child labour only in factories; it left untouched child labour on the farms, and indeed any form of child labour under direct parental order. Since the Act had been fomented primarily by agricultural landowners, there is some substance in the accusation by contemporary millowners that its real purpose was not the welfare of children but the subjection of industry; Lord Shaftesbury did not abolish child labour on his farms. W. Cooke Taylor, in his *Factories and the Factory System* (1844), observed: 'Persons enter a mill, or suppose that they have done so, they see, or imagine to themselves, the figures of the little piecers and cleaners employed in their monotonous routine, when the sun is high in heaven . . . and they think how much more delightful would have been the gambol of the free limbs on the hill-side, the inhaling of the fresh breeze, the sight of the green mead, with its spangles of butter-cups and daisies, the song of the bird, and the humming of the bee! But they should compare the aspect of the youthful operatives with other sights which they must have met in the course of their experience . . . we have seen children perishing from sheer hunger in the mud-hovel, or in the ditch by the way-side, where a few sods and withered boughs had formed a hut, compared with which a wigwam were a palace.' 'The children engaged in the mills', concluded Taylor, 'are better paid, and work less. . . There are no tasks imposed on young persons in factories that are anything near so laborious as hand-weeding corn, hay-making, stone-picking, potato-picking, or bean-chopping.'

The partial collapse of British agriculture in the 1870s, with a resulting decline in the rate of investment in rural improvement, meant that this situation continued largely unchanged into the Edwardian period; George Sturt, writing under the pseudonym 'George Bourne' in *Change in the Village* (1912), reported that it was not uncommon to see boys carrying coal 'at an age when boys in better circumstances are hardly allowed out alone', and school inspectors on the eve of the First World War found it virtually impossible to enforce school attendance if the parents said their children were needed on the farm. Nothing of this is hinted in the work of the later cottage-garden painters; the happy child playing in the cottage garden became a stock image. The disparity between the picturesque image and the squalid reality, complained about by the Victorian reformers, remained a subject for complaint at the beginning of the twentieth century, as witness the following passage from W.H. Hudson's *Land's End* (1908): 'One day last summer a lady visitor staying in the neighbourhood came to where he was doing some work and burst out in praise of the place, and told him she envied him his home in the dearest, sweetest, loveliest spot on earth. "That's what you think, ma'am," he returned, "because you're here for a week or two in summer when it's fine and the heath in bloom. Now I think it's the poorest, ugliest, horriblest place in the whole world, because I've got to live on it and get my living out of it."'

Some aspects of the typical cottage garden painting, then, are the results of idealization, the suppression of squalid reality. But a genuine transformation of cottage gardens was in fact taking place during the Victorian period. An early example can be seen in Thomas Bernard's *Account of a Cottage and Garden near Tadcaster* (1797): Briton Abbot, a Yorkshire labourer, dispossessed by enclosure, was granted a quarter of an acre by a local squire, built a cottage, and planted the garden

GATHERING LILAC
Myles Birket Foster

with apple, plum, and apricot trees, gooseberry and currant bushes, and vegetables. He was soon producing forty bushels of potatoes annually. Bernard's pamphlet recommended the provision of cottage gardens as an alternative to the workhouse. Loudon's *Encyclopaedia of Cottage, Farm, and Villa Architecture* (1833) provided a model for many landowners in the improvement of their estates, and one of Loudon's recommendations was the provision of gardens. Birket Foster's paintings, with their vegetable gardens and comparative absence of flowers, may be taken as representing the first stage in the increase of cottage gardens, in which their primary function was to augment the labourers' food supply. Many landowners, however, wanting their estate villages to serve as an advertisement for their taste, insisted on the provision and maintenance of flower gardens as well, and it was gardens like these that were more likely to attract the artist, as the gardener Alexander Forsyth complained in the *Gardeners' Chronicle* in 1872: 'Cottage gardening, like cottage life, is mispresented by authors unacquainted with the subject, who deal in fine writing, and take one-sided views, and give the thing a sentimental dash for the sake of effect. When we read of the allotment gardens near Nottingham being rich in the choicest kinds of Roses, we mistake the thing altogether; for the capital embarked in such gardens is a clear proof that the owner is a man of some substance... no ordinary tenant-farmer could be asked to imitate [such] things...'. The question whether flowers, and if so what flowers, had any place in the gardens of labourers' cottages was much debated.

One way or another, however, cottage gardens were on the increase throughout the mid-nineteenth century. Fifty years ago, said Thomas Hardy's mother in the 1850s, 'Yonder garden-plots and orchards were uncultivated slopes O'ergrown with bramble bushes, furze and thorn...' ('Domicilium'). And the great gardener Donald Beaton, writing in 1852, described the area around his own retirement cottage in Surbiton: 'In a circle of no more than two miles in diameter, round my house, there are as many cottage gardens, if not more, of the best class, than are to be met with in the same space in any other part of the country, and they were all made and planted within the last twenty years.'

FEEDING THE CAT
Myles Birket Foster

The most famous of Victorian 'cottage art-ists', and perhaps the name most closely associated with Victorian watercolours, is Myles Birket Foster. He was born in North Shields in 1825 and was educated in Quaker schools when his parents moved to London in 1830. His artistic aptitude was evident from an early age, and he was soon apprenticed to the wood engraver Peter Landells. Until 1850 he worked as an illustrator, making designs for such magazines as the *Illustrated London News*.

In the 1850s he taught himself to paint in watercolour and became proficient in a short time. After 1860 he exhibited regularly, show-ing over 400 works at the Old Watercolour Society, to which he was elected a full member in 1862. Despite his association with English pastoral scenes, he travelled widely and did many watercolours abroad; Charles Seely of Nottingham commissioned him to paint a series of fifty Venetian views, for which he was paid a fee of £5,000.

Much of Birket Foster's work was done in Surrey, and particularly around Witley, where for several years he spent his summers in a 'picturesque cottage' called Tigbourne. Eventually he decided to build his own house there, called The Hill, which he decorated with the help of the Pre-Raphaelite artists William Morris and Edward Burne-Jones. This soon became established as a regular visiting-place for other cottage artists, such as Helen Al-lingham, who lived nearby.

FETCHING WATER
Myles Birket Foster

A KENTISH COTTAGE
Helen Allingham

Helen Allingham (sometimes referred to by her maiden name Paterson) was born near Burton-on-Trent, the daughter of a doctor. She studied at the Birmingham School of Design and in 1867 went to the Royal Academy Schools, where she was greatly influenced by the work of Birket Foster and Frederick Walker. She began her career by working as an illustrator for the *Graphic* and *Cornhill* magazines. For a time she and her fellow illustrator Kate Greenaway lived in Hampstead and went on painting excursions together. Her description of these jaunts was published in M.H.

Spielmann and G.S. Layard's book *Kate Greenaway* (1905): 'During the summer . . . we continued our outdoor work together, generally taking an early train from Finchley Road to Pinner, for the day. She [Greenaway] was always scrupulously thoughtful for the convenience and feelings of the owners of the farms and cottages we wished to paint, with the consequence that we were made welcome to sit in the garden or orchard where others were refused admittance.'

In 1874 she married the Irish poet William Allingham, and through him soon made the

acquaintance of Carlyle, Tennyson, and Ruskin. In *The Art of England* (1884), Ruskin was to talk about her gift for the representation of 'the gesture, character, and humour of charming children in country landscapes'. In 1881, the Allinghams moved to Witley, the Surrey village where Birket Foster lived; it was only then that the cottage and its garden emerged as her principal theme. Most of her cottage pictures, like these examples, were painted in Kent and Surrey. Between them, Birket Foster and Allingham made Witley a centre for artists inspired by the cottage theme.

SHERE
Helen Allingham

GIRL OUTSIDE COTTAGE
Helen Allingham

GIRL BY A STREAM BEFORE A HOUSE
Helen Allingham

A good insight into Helen Allingham's technique was given by Marcus B. Huish in his book *The Happy England of Helen Allingham* (1903): 'when this book was proposed to Mrs Allingham her chief objection was her certainty that no process could reproduce her drawings satisfactorily. Her method of work was, she believed, entirely opposed to mechanical reproduction ... obtaining effects by rubbing, scrubbing and scratching... Now nowhere are these methods of Mrs Allingham's more util-ised, and with greater effect, than in her drawings of flower-gardens... The plan adopted a generation or so ago was first to draw and paint the flowers and then the foliage. This method left the flowers isolated objects and the foliage without substantiality... [Allingham's flowers are] carved out of a background ... and left as white paper, all their drawing and modelling being achieved by a dexterous use of the knife and a wetted and rubbed surface... There are no badly pencilled outlines, and the blooms blend amongst themselves and grow naturally out of their foliage.' The success of this technique can be judged from these two pictures; its disadvantage is a frequent blurring of detail within the flower itself.

For many years her watercolours were ignored and even twenty years ago one could buy them for as little as £4. Today, however, the tremendous, although belated, revival of interest in many prodigiously talented Victorians have made her work eagerly sought after.

MOTHER AND CHILD AND GEESE OUTSIDE A SMALL HOUSE
Charles Low

PLAYING OUTSIDE THE COTTAGE
Caroline Sharpe

Birket Foster and Allingham made Witley a centre for artists inspired by the cottage theme; one of these was Charles Low, who eventually settled there in 1896. He was a highly competent artist, as the charming picture on the left demonstrates, and although he did not achieve great fame during his lifetime he did become a member of the Royal Society of British Artists, exhibiting regularly at the Royal Academy as well as the Royal Hibernian Academy.

Caroline Paterson (who later became Caroline Sharpe, after marrying the etcher Sutton Sharpe) has always lived under the shadow of her more illustrious sister Helen Allingham, by whom she was undoubtedly influenced. A fine artist in her own right, she had a good sense of colour and was a gifted portrayer of young children.

Her pictures tend to be more sentimental than her sister's, but in general the work of the Witley circle is characterized by its detailed observation and is unsentimental by comparison with other cottage painters. Our century, however, has tended to blur these distinctions. In 1931 W. Graham Robertson wrote of Allingham's work in *Time Was*: 'Her lovely little transcripts of the Surrey lanes and woodlands ... are delights to the eye and lasting memorials of the fast-vanishing beauty of our countryside. In a few more years they will seem visions of a lost Fairyland, a dream world fabulous and remote as Lyonesse or Atlantis, but they are no false mirages but beautiful truth; few painters have ever penetrated so close to the sound of the English Country.'

THE OBEDIENT DOG
Charles Edward Wilson

The contrast between the work of the Witley circle and that of their successors can be seen immediately in this picture by Charles Edward Wilson. It is not known when Wilson was born but his birthplace was Whitwell, Nottingham. He exhibited from 1891, mainly at the Royal Society of Painters in Watercolour, and he died in 1936. It is surprising that so few biographical details are recorded when one considers the excellence of his pictures and his accomplishments as a watercolourist. He developed a very precise technique and observed his subjects closely; often he introduced children and animals into his pictures, and there is no doubt that he enjoyed creating unashamedly nostalgic and sentimental images, such as the expectant begging dog shown here. Notice the pelargoniums on the window ledge inside the cottage, brought in for protection from frost as autumn approaches.

In Tyndale's picture it is definitely spring-time, as the blossom on the fruit tree and the colourful border with pansies, tulips and wallflowers proclaim. The artist (*fl.* 1900–25) was a friend of Helen Allingham and a cousin of the better-known Walter Tyndale. He lived in Gunnersbury and, in the 1920s, at Worthing. He exhibited quite extensively at, among other venues, the Walker Art Gallery, Liverpool, and the Bristol Academy. In 1903 he won a Bristol Art Union Prize, and in 1909 twenty-four of his watercolours were reproduced in *Worcestershire* by A.G. Bradley.

OUTSIDE A COTTAGE
Thomas Nicholson Tyndale

IN A WARWICKSHIRE BYWAY, LITTLE MILTON
Henry John Sylvester Stannard

GIRL LOOKING AT A COTTAGE
Henry John Sylvester Stannard

As in these two watercolours, cottage gardens in Stannard's pictures tend to be planted with a predictable range of delphiniums, hollyhocks, asters, and climbing roses – plants recommended in Victorian manuals for cottagers, and eventually to be regarded as staple 'cottage garden plants'. Genuinely poor cottagers would probably have depended largely on their landlords, local vicars, and the like for seeds and plants, so that range of garden stock would not have been wide in the gardens which so many of Stannard's pictures depict.

Henry John Sylvester Stannard came from a large family of artists. He was born in London in 1870 and educated in Bedford, where he spent most of his life. His father, Henry Stannard, was a sporting artist and encouraged his son to paint from an early age; he exhibited his first picture, 'A Note on the Ouse', at the Royal Society of British Artists, and was elected a member of this Society in 1909.

In 1905 he received permission from Queen Alexandra to work at Sandringham, and spent much time painting the Queen's gardens and woods. In 1906 she bought one of his watercolours entitled 'Sandringham Church', and towards the end of the year she commissioned a number of watercolours, one of which was presented to the Queen of Norway. Queen Alexandra became so enthusiastic about Stannard's garden scenes that she bought more than twenty of his pictures. Royal patronage also came from abroad; in 1909 Marie Louise of Schleswig-Holstein bought one of his works. Such patronage led the *Arts Review* in 1908 to describe Stannard as 'one of the best-known English artists of our time', and soon many of his works were being used to illustrate books or were made into prints.

KNOWLE HILL
Sir Ernest Waterlow

Samuel Towers's picture illustrates the growing popularity of the Cotswolds at this time as an area of surviving rural traditions. In the 1880s an artists' colony of sorts, with John Singer Sargent and Alfred Parsons as prominent figures, grew up at Broadway, not far from the village portrayed here; by the turn of the century Arts-and-Crafts architects like Guy Dawber and the Barnsley brothers had moved their practices to the area, and C. R. Ashbee was to move his Guild of Handicrafts to Chipping Campden in 1902. The Cotswolds were thus coming to rival rural Surrey as a centre for cottage painting.

Towers was born at Bolton in Lancashire on 17 September 1862. He exhibited at the Royal Academy from 1884, painting some rather beautiful watercolours with a fresh, natural approach to colour and a good understanding of light; indeed, in this example one is left firmly with the impression of a hot sunny day. He lived for some years at Harrington in Worcestershire and died in 1943.

Ernest Waterlow (1850–1910) was born in London and studied art at Heidelberg and Lausanne. He entered the Royal Academy Schools in 1872 and the following year won the Turner Gold Medal. In 1894 he was made a member of the Royal Watercolour Society, becoming its president in 1897 and a Royal Academician in 1903. In 1902 he was knighted. His watercolours show a fluid technique and a great understanding of the effects of light.

VILLAGE CROSS, ASHTON-UNDER-HILL, NEAR EVESHAM
Samuel Towers

GOING TO MARKET
Arthur Claude Strachan

The image of the cottage, as these pictures testify, was a potent one in the late nineteenth century. Its popularity can be seen in terms of a reaction against what was perceived as the ugliness of the Industrial Revolution, as exemplified by the slum conditions of Manchester or Coalbrookdale. The simplicity and beauty of the past seemed still discoverable in rural villages and footpaths where, as John Scott of Amwell had written in the 1780s in his *Amoebean Eclogues*:

In shady lanes the foxglove bells appear,
And golden spikes the downy mulleins rear;
The enclosure ditch luxuriant mallows hide;
And branchy succory crowds the pathway wide.

'You cannot wonder, then, that these fields are popular places of resort at every holiday time', wrote Mrs Gaskell in *Mary Barton*, as the urban population arrived to witness 'the country business of haymaking, ploughing, &c... such pleasant mysteries for townspeople to watch'.

Rural beauty, however, was in the eye of the beholder, as W.H. Hudson's tramp explained in *Afoot in England*: '"Very fine, very beautiful all this" – waving his hand to indicate the hedge, its rich tangle of purple-red stems and coloured leaves, and scarlet fruit and silvery old-man's-beard. "An artist enjoys seeing this sort of thing, ... But when it comes to a man tramping twenty or thirty miles a day on an empty belly, looking for work which he can't find, he doesn't see it in quite the same way."'

SHEEP OUTSIDE A COTTAGE
Arthur Claude Strachan

CUTTING CABBAGES
Myles Birket Foster

CHILDREN OUTSIDE A COTTAGE
Henry John Sylvester Stannard

The treatment of children acts as a barometer for sentimentality in cottage painting. Child labour is glossed over by most painters of cottage scenes, but it was a continuing reality of the countryside. W. Cooke Taylor, in *Factories and the Factory System* (1844), observed: 'There are many who will doubt or disbelieve the fact that mill-work is preferred to agricultural labour by young persons; their imaginations have been too long dazzled by Arcadian pictures of rural life, for them to take the trouble of attending to sober realities. One great cause of the prevalent delusion is, that agricultural labour is rarely witnessed by casual spectators except during fine weather.'

Birket Foster's children are more likely than those of any other cottage artist to be seen working, or preparing for their future lives by watching others work, as in the watercolour on the left. Note the presence of pinks and roses among the cabbages in this picture, representing an attempt by the cottager to brighten up this otherwise utilitarian garden. This honest depiction of labour was somewhat softened even in Helen Allingham's work, and most of her successors restricted themselves to children playing idly in the cottage garden. This focus on play, as seen in Stannard's picture, created an image of children as the inheritors of a rural paradise. Yet at the height of fashion for cottage pictures, George Bourne remarked that cottagers' children were psychologically impoverished, 'extremely ill-supplied with subjects to think about', and that their play was empty and limited in imagination by comparison with that of town children.

THE THATCHER
Henry John Sylvester Stannard

The more substantial cottages were protected from the road by hedges, fences or ditches. Cottage hedges have been little studied, and it is difficult to determine to what extent they were deliberately planted, and to what extent they began as fencing or as ditch banks which were invaded by vegetation during periods of neglect. The hedges of the eighteenth and nineteenth centuries tended to be of single species, most commonly hawthorn; older ones, however, such as that shown here, tended to become conglomerations of different species.

By the beginning of the nineteenth century, thatch was being promoted for cottages because of its picturesque and old-fashioned appearance; such pioneering model villages as Milton Abbas in the 1780s and Blaise Hamlet in the 1800s used thatched roofs. Victorian reformers, however, were not so enthusiastic; Alexander Mackay described a typical Buckinghamshire cottage in the *Morning Chronicle* (24 October 1849): 'The wall ... is composed of a species of imperfect sandstone, which is fast crumbling to decay... The thatch is thickly encrusted with a bright green vegetation, which, together with the appearance of the trees and the mason-work around, well attests the prevailing humidity of the atmosphere.' The various sanitary commissions which investigated rural housing in the nineteenth century tended to condemn thatch as maintenance-intensive and as providing a harbour for vermin.

AT THE COTTAGE GATE
Helen Allingham

GIRL WITH DOVES BEFORE A COTTAGE
Arthur Claude Strachan

When labourers' cottages were equipped with gardens, or when their settlement was furnished with allotments at a distance from the cottages, their primary use was to grow food. Up until the 1890s, manuals on cottage gardening were primarily devoted to instruction in fruit and vegetable cultivation, and flowers occupied a very subordinate position. By the early nineteenth century the potato had become the staple crop for the poor, but reformers and the writers of such manuals tried to broaden the range of food crops available to the cottagers by recommending different sorts of apple and pear trees, currant and other bushes for training on walls, and a greater variety of leaf vegetables. By the end of the century these instructions had taken effect, as Flora Thompson recorded in *Lark Rise* (1939), recalling village life in the 1880s: 'The energy they brought to their gardening after a hard day's work in the fields was marvellous. They grudged no effort and seemed never to tire.... Proud as they were of their celery, peas and beans, cauliflowers and marrows, and fine as were the specimens they could show of these, their potatoes were their special care, for they had to grow enough to last the year round. They grew all the old-fashioned varieties – ashleaf kidney, early rose, American rose, magnum bonum, and the huge misshaped white elephant. Everybody knew the elephant was an unsatisfactory potato ... but it produced tubers of such astonishing size that none of the men could resist the temptation to plant it.'

Pictures of cottage and kitchen gardens tend to stress the presence of cabbages more than other vegetables – possibly as more interesting to paint. Even the more floriferous garden in Strachan's picture boasts a clump of cabbages and a pair of fruit trees on the right. Those labourers who had gardens generally could not afford not to use them to augment their food supply, although George Bourne thought that 'he is a fortunate man, or an unusually industrious one, who can make his gardening worth more than two shillings a week to him in food. There must be many cottages ... where the yield of the garden is scarcely half that value.'

THE COTTAGE GARDEN
Myles Birket Foster

WOMAN OUTSIDE COTTAGE WITH DUCKS
Arthur Claude Strachan

A COTTAGE GARDEN
Lilian Stannard

Where flowers were grown in cottage gardens, it was usually for a practical purpose, whether for their medicinal qualities or as scented plants for concealing unpleasant smells. Mrs Gaskell, in *Mary Barton*, described a farmhouse garden of the early Victorian period: 'The porch of this farm-house is covered by a rose-tree; and the little garden surrounding it is crowded with a medley of old-fashioned herbs and flowers, planted long ago, when the garden was the only druggist's shop within reach, and allowed to grow in scrambling and wild luxuriance – roses, lavender, sage, balm (for tea), rosemary, pinks and wall-flowers, onions and jessamine, in the most republican and indiscriminate order.' Roses were long regarded as an all-purpose medicinal plant; sage was used for digestive upsets, rosemary for headaches, wall-flowers for nervous disorders, jessamine for coughs; onions had once been used as an aphrodisiac and later, more commonly, as an antiseptic; the perfume of lavender could be used to counteract faintness as well as to freshen the cottage atmosphere. Add to this list other medicinal plants such as foxgloves and stocks, and a range of plants for bees, and it is apparent that the ornamental quality of the cottage garden, later the subject of much praise and attention, was largely an accidental by-product. Nevertheless, it is clear from these two charming watercolours, that these plants were quite decorative enough to attract artists such as Stannard and Strachan.

ASHOW CHURCH
Thomas Mackay

CHAPTER II

THE COTTAGE GARDEN TRANSFORMED

HE landowner's model village, in which the cottagers were expected to cultivate flower gardens for display, was greeted by men like J.C. Loudon with mixed feelings. He would have preferred gardens that were useful and productive for the labourers; however, 'though we find fault with villages ornamented in these ways, we are still glad to see them; because any kind of alteration in the dwellings and gardens of country labourers can hardly fail to be an improvement'.

George Bourne, writing at the beginning of the twentieth century, noted the frequency of the cottagers' attempts to introduce some degree of ornament into their surroundings: 'Amidst the pitiful shabbiness which prevailed may be found many little signs that the delight in comely things would go far if it dared. There is hardly a garden in the village, I think, which does not contain a corner or a strip given over unthriftily, not to useful vegetables, but to daffodils or carnations or dahlias, or to the plants of sweet scent and pleasant names, like rosemary and lavender, and balm, and mignonette. And not seldom a weekly tenant, desirous of beauty, goes farther, takes his chance of losing his pains; nails up against his doorway some makeshift structure of fir-poles to be a porch, sowing nasturtiums or sweet-peas to cover it with their short-lived beauty; or he markes out under his window some little trumpery border to serve instead of a box-hedge as a safeguard to his flowers. [An evicted family] found refuge in a hovel which stood right against a public pathway. And, although it was an encroachment, within a week a twelve-inch strip of the pathway was dug up under the cottage eaves, and fenced in with a low fencing of sticks roughly nailed together. Within this narrow space were planted chrysanthemums rescued from the previous home; and when the fence gave way – as it did before the chrysanthemums flowered – big stones and brickbats were laid in its place. Considered as decoration, the result was a failure; it was the product of an hour's work in which despair and bitterness had all but killed the people's hope; but that it was done at all is almost enough to prove my point.'

By the mid-nineteenth century it was being noted that the better-off cottagers were imitating the current gardening fashions and planting bedding plants. Indeed, the pelargonium, treated as a pot plant for the window, was to become almost a staple of cottage gardens; Bourne's phraseology, in trying to dispel the illusion that the life of the cottage housewife was 'an idyll of samplers and geraniums in cottage windows', shows how widespread it had become. Most gardening writers thought that half-hardy plants were too labour-intensive to be worthwhile in a cottage garden, but the cottagers persisted.

By the 1860s and 1870s, however, the hardy perennials recommended in books like Robert Adamson's *Cottage Garden* (1851) were coming into fashion as part of the new trend in historical revivalism: the attempt to make planting as well as layout historically accurate. William Robinson's claim that during the fashion for bedding many gardens were to be seen without a single hardy plant, was used to promote interest in cottage gardens as places where these neglected annuals and perennials survived. In fact, annuals and hardy perennials provided half the volume of the nursery trade throughout the Victorian period; gardening writers consistently urged them as the mainstay for smaller gardens which could not afford the expense of protected cultivation for tender plants throughout the winter. When the gardening magazines actually named specific plants which were believed to be lost from cultivation, they tended to be not the well-known herbaceous perennials but the old florists' flowers – the varieties of auricula, carnation and the like that had been raised for competition in the eighteenth and early nineteenth centuries. Nonetheless, an architect like John D. Sedding, in his *Garden-Craft Old and New* (1891), could write that 'The common flowers of the cottager's garden tell of centuries of collaboration' between man and nature, and these stories of loss and rescue reinforced the idea that the cottage garden was something of immesurable antiquity.

This idea was reinforced by a confusion over what counted as a cottage. William Robinson's praise for the cottage garden, when specific examples were offered, implied not the labourer's garden but rather the old farmhouse or small manor house, or a parsonage like Gilbert White's at Selborne. The later literature followed his example: the cottage garden, when promoted as a model for design or planting, simply meant the garden of the smaller rural house. Sometimes this confusion seems to have been deliberate. Helen Allingham, for example, was a close friend of Tennyson, and frequently painted pictures of his gardens. One of these, depicting a corner of the walled garden and dairy on his estate at Farringford, was published in D.C. Calthrop's book *The Charm of Gardens* (1910) under the title 'The Cottage Garden'.

Experiments with mixed borders, the older tradition of grouping plants without the massing of colours, had continued all through the period when massed bedding was fashionable – promoted, indeed, by the same writers, like Donald Beaton, who wrote in the 1850s that 'Mixed borders we all have, or ought to have', and who regarded the planning of the mixed border as the great unsolved problem of gardening art. All this was forgotten in the renewed enthusiasm over herbaceous plants late in the century; rural gardens with herbaceous planting, even though they may have owed their style to the weekly advice Beaton dispensed in the *Cottage Gardener* magazine, were proclaimed as the inheritors of an old tradition. So, ironically, it was the mixed style of the early Victorian period which came to be promoted as the 'cottage garden style', and eventually claimed as something of immeasurable antiquity.

The desire to see the cottage garden as a little pocket of undisturbed tradition was frequently accompanied by an aesthetic liking for the traditional crafts of cottage life, whether building techniques, furniture and household equipment, or clothing. Gertrude Jekyll's *Old West Surrey* was a plea for the cottager to remain simple and uncorrupted by modern life; even sanitary improvement had to be reconciled with the aesthetic value of the unimproved cottages: 'One has to admit that modern-built cottages are warmer, drier, and more healthy; but, to those who feel as I do, it is a matter of never-ending regret that those who build them have so little care for local tradition . . .' (*Home and Garden*, 1900). A genuine villager like George Bourne, on the other hand, set his face against 'those self-conscious revivals of peasant arts which are now being recommended to the poor by a certain type of philanthropist'.

CLEMATIS COTTAGE
Ernest Albert Chadwick

The most ornamental and flowery of cottage gardens were those created by landowners for their tenants, as evidence of their own taste. In the 1830s, Gregory Gregory of Harlaxton created such a village for his estate, which was held up as a model by Loudon in his *Gardener's Magazine* for 1840. 'Every garden has been laid out and planted by Mr. Gregory's gardener; creepers and climbers being introduced in proper places, in such a manner as that no two gardens are planted with the same climbers,' 'Proper places' – an important point, for Loudon was quite prepared to attack the use of climbing plants on cottages, which 'if ornamental, is so at the expense of comfort; the creepers, by which the trelliswork is covered, darkening the rooms, and encouraging insects'.

By the 1870s, however, manuals on gardening were suggesting plants for training on cottage walls. E. Hobday, in his *Cottage Gardening* (1877), listed clematis – seen in both these pictures, accompanied by a climbing rose in Helen Allingham's – Virginia creeper, jasmines, ivy, cotoneaster, box, berberis, and such exotics as 'Canary Creeper, and other Tropaeolums', *Cobaea scandens*, *Maurandia barclayana* and *M. lophospermum* as suitable – with a wider range of convulvulus, saxifrages, sedums, pelargoniums, vincas, and even the rat's-tail cactus for use in hanging baskets.

GIRL WITH DOVES OUTSIDE A COTTAGE
Helen Allingham

COTTAGE IN DEVON
Robert Walker Macbeth

BEEHIVES
Frank Walton

The role of flowers in the cottage garden gradually increased as the nineteenth century wore on, and as the writers of manuals for cottagers placed greater importance on instruction in flower-gardening. Robert Adamson, in *The Cottage Garden* (1851), was still recommending medicinal herbs for the floral part of the garden; nonetheless, he finds room for a large range of ornamental plants, mostly bulbs or perennials, but including several fashionable exotics: eschscholtzias, nemophilas, fuchsias, dahlias, and bedding plants such as calceolarias and verbenas. His planting instructions are fairly elementary, e.g. place the smaller plants in front of the taller ones. Later in the century, things have become more sophisticated. Edward Hobday, in *Cottage Gardening* (1877), and the anonymous writer of *Cottage Gardening* (1894), assume that many cottagers will have at least a couple of frames in the garden, if not a small greenhouse. Hobday recommends box, aucuba, and ivy as shrubs; both writers, and Albert Kerridge in *Early Lessons in Cottage Gardening* (1907), recognize chrysanthemums, fuchsias and pelargoniums as probably the most popular of plants grown by cottagers.

All four manuals agree on a short-list, which we can take as the basis for the Victorian cottage flower garden: snowdrops, crocus, hyacinths, tulips, daffodils; polyanthus, pansies, stocks, asters, mignonette, sweet peas, pinks, carnations, roses, lilies, gladioli; chrysanthemums, dahlias, pelargoniums and fuchsias as window plants. Straw skeps for bees were commonly placed on individual stands, as shown here, or in rows on benches. Most Victorian manuals tried to introduce a higher technological level into cottagers' beekeeping, but the enthusiasts of the cottage garden cult naturally preferred to depict more traditional methods of working.

WOMEN SEWING OUTSIDE A COTTAGE
David Woodlock

By the end of the nineteenth century, the promotion of cottagers' gardens was no longer limited to estate owners and philanthropists; local government was beginning to take a hand. Kent and Surrey County Councils were the pioneers; John Wright built up their programmes of school gardening and further education for adults – these councils, wrote Dean Hole, 'not only teach the husband how to grow his vegetables, but they show his wife how to cook them. In the last year 515 meetings, held at 14 centres, have been attended by 12,861 pupils.' Kent and Surrey were also among the first counties to organize Cottage Gardeners' Shows, awarding prizes for produce; to qualify as a cottager for such competitions, one had to be a working-class person who 'must not receive any professional assistance or paid labour in the cultivation of his garden'.

Dean Hole, writing in *Our Gardens* (1902), urged that every labourer 'should have appletree, plum-tree, and cherry-tree, his bushes of gooseberries and currants, his potatoes and greens, in addition to his garden of flowers'. He and various other writers emphasized the role of the local clergyman in encouraging an interest in gardening among the villagers. This horticultural enthusiasm went hand-in-hand with sanitary redevelopment; Robert Adamson in 1851 had urged that every cottage garden should have a dung-pit and liquid manure tank; the late Victorian attempt to promote the earth closet in rural areas increased many cottagers' facilities for ready fertilizer. The presence of pots for ornamental plants in both these pictures – especially the prolific collection on the left – suggests a horticultural enthusiasm of the sort that Hole was encouraging.

PICKING FLOWERS
Charles Edward Wilson

GIRL WITH DOG OUTSIDE COTTAGE
Arthur Claude Strachan

Horticultural sophistication met with a mixed response from the cottagers' betters. Cottagers were regularly urged to restrict themselves to annuals and perennials that did not need protected cultivation. Questions of taste as well as practicality entered such discussions, however; in 1853 J.S. Barty growled in *Blackwood's Magazine* that cottage gardens were getting too conscious of fashion, and this complaint was to be repeated. With the burgeoning interest in 'old-fashioned flowers' in the 1860s and 1870s, it became common to regard cottage gardens as little enclaves of tradition, where such flowers ought to survive untouched by the ravages of fashion. Mrs Loftie commented wryly on the situation: 'It is often amusing to trace a fashion as it percolates downwards... Cottagers now try to fill their little plots with geraniums and calceolarias, which they are obliged to keep indoors at great inconvenience to themselves and loss of light to their rooms. Meantime my lady at the Court is hunting the nursery grounds for London Pride and gentianella to make edgings in her wilderness, and for the fair tall rockets, the cabbage roses, and the nodding columbines which her pensioners have discarded and thrown away.'

Robert Adamson had recommended hollyhocks, asters, – as shown in Strachan's picture – carnations, pinks, sweet williams, wallflowers, primroses, rocket, stocks, sweet peas, pansies, phlox, delphiniums, spiraeas, potentillas, and aquilegias for the cottage garden; these, together with sunflowers (as shown in Woodlock's picture), were to be thought of by the next generation of garden writers as the archetypal cottage plants – whatever the cottagers themselves may have preferred.

PICKING FLOWERS
David Woodlock

GARDENING OUTSIDE THE COTTAGE
Arthur Claude Strachan

As the image of the cottage garden and that of the old-fashioned garden merged, it becomes difficult to determine exactly what is meant by a cottage in gardening literature. The buildings depicted here could both qualify as cottages in some nineteenth-century usages, but neither is a labourer's cottage, and neither would have met the conditions of a cottage gardeners' competition.

The late eighteenth century, among its other forms of pastoral play-acting, had seen the rise of a fashion for calling rural villas 'cottages', and the phrase '*cottage orné*' could mean either a decorative estate cottage, like John Adey Repton's old English gatekeeper's cottage at Woburn Abbey, or a small house in a picturesque style. The painting on the right falls into the latter category. That above, with its outbuildings and tiled courtyard, is a farmhouse or perhaps even a small manor house. It is this sort of building that is depicted as a cottage in William Robinson's *English Flower Garden*; although that volume praises the cottage garden, none of the examples illustrated could unambiguously be called a labourer's cottage – even when Sir Richard Owen's 'cottage' (i.e. villa) at Sheen is overlooked.

COMING HOME
Arthur Claude Strachan

LARGE COTTAGE BY A RIVER
Arthur Claude Strachan

DOVES BEFORE COTTAGE
Arthur Claude Strachan

By the 1880s, the cottage garden was being proclaimed as an indigenous gardening style. The first major propagandist for this approach was William Robinson, whose anthology *The English Flower Garden*, published in 1883, uses the cottage garden as an alternative to the high Victorian garden with its emphasis on architecture and seasonal bedding: 'English cottage gardens are never bare and seldom ugly. Those who look at sea or sky or wood see beauty that no art can show; but among the things made by man nothing is prettier than an English cottage garden, and they often teach lessons that "great" gardeners should learn, and are pretty from snowdrop time till the Fuschia bushes bloom nearly into winter...

'What is the secret of the cottage garden's charms?... it is the absence of any pretentious "plan" which lets the flowers tell their story to the heart. The walks are only what are needed, and so we see only the earth and its blossoms.' The closely planted hollyhocks, heleniums, phlox, lavender, and asters of 'Doves before Cottage' illustrate Robinson's desired avoidance of bareness. The gardener and plant hunter F.W. Burbridge, in a contribution to the 1895 edition of *The English Flower Garden*, continued Robinson's campaign: '[The] simple cottage in an out-of-the-way corner may also serve to teach us a little of the truth and subtlety of the landscape gardener's art. Here are no adventitious features nor complicated designs; no mop-headed Roses nor carpet beds to disturb the sweet repose of the bit of greensward as it dips gently and naturally from the door; and yet all the elements of the best art are there – the clear sky, the lingering sunshine, the trees, the turf, and the house itself, all combining to afford us a scene of typical English beauty essentially home-like in its character...'. As the emphasis on turf and greensward makes clear, Burbidge's ideal cottage is not that of a poor cottager, but rather a larger house like that in the picture on the left, which appears to have its own orchard.

TORCH LILIES
Ernest Albert Chadwick

Robinson's campaign to increase the popularity of the cottage garden was continued by Gertrude Jekyll, with special emphasis on the role of cottage gardens in preserving plants that had fallen from fashion. She wrote in her first book, *Wood and Garden* (1899): 'I have learnt much from the little cottage gardens that help to make our English waysides the prettiest in the temperate world. One can hardly go into the smallest cottage garden without learning or observing something new. It may be some two plants growing beautifully together by some happy chance, or a pretty mixed tangle of creepers, or something that one always thought must have a south wall doing better on an east one. But eye and brain must be alert to receive the impression and studious to store it. . .

'Some of the most delightful of all gardens are the little strips in front of roadside cottages. They have a simple and tender charm that one may look for in vain in gardens of greater pretension. And the old garden flowers seem to know that there they are seen at their best; for where else can one see such Wallflowers, or Double Daisies, or White Rose bushes; such clustering masses of perennial Peas, or such well-kept flowery edgings of Pink, or thrift, or London Pride?' Note that Jekyll is merely claiming that these plants were in their proper setting around the cottage, not that they had disappeared from cultivation elsewhere; but the legend was rapidly coming to be part of the accepted lore of the cottage garden. Some of Jekyll's favourite flowers – such as *Kniphofia* (torch lilies or red-hot pokers) – were absorbed into the category of cottage garden plants, even though they had not been evident in previous literature on the subject.

THE VISITORS
Arthur Claude Strachan

PICKING FLOWERS
David Woodlock

While horticultural writers like Robinson and Jekyll were praising the planting of cottage gardens, garden architects like Inigo Thomas and Thomas Mawson were holding up the cottage garden as a model for traditional design, Mawson praising its topiary and hedges (above) and Thomas its box-edged compartments (right). The fact that the categories of 'cottage garden plants' and 'old-fashioned plants' overlapped so heavily – the hollyhocks, phlox, dianthus, poppies and lavender shown in these pictures could be placed in either category – was an additional advantage for the historically-minded gardener trying to recreate the past.

It was left for Charles Thonger, however, in his *Book of the Cottage Garden* (1909), to make the highest claims for the cottage garden, offering it as an alternative to the grander sort of revivalist garden, and dismissing any suggestion that cottagers had made gardens by imitating those of their betters: 'But supposing after all that these things are not so; that the cottage garden, far from being an insignificant attempt to ape the splendours of more pretentious pleasure grounds, is in reality our nearest available approach to the ideal. . . .

'Here is no straining after effect, no surrender to the dictates of passing fashion, no meaningless attempt to introduce into an environment utterly foreign to them, styles and mannerisms borrowed from other countries. Here we shall seek in vain the statuary and vases which, according so admirably with the stately dignity of those memory-haunted gardens of Italy, distort and make hideous the expensive ''gardens'' which certain architects have planned for English parvenus. . .

'In short, the average cottage garden *is* a garden, not a piece of ground littered with a medley of rubbish.'

GIRL AND KITTEN BEFORE COTTAGE
Arthur Claude Strachan

COTTAGE
Theresa Stannard

GIRL WITH CAT AND DOVES OUTSIDE A COTTAGE
Arthur Claude Strachan

Painters as well as garden writers played their part in promoting what was coming to be called the 'cottage garden style.' One of the most prolific of these was Arthur Claude Strachan (1865-*c*.1935). He was born in Edinburgh and spent most of his life in Liverpool, exhibiting many pictures at the Walker Art Gallery and four at the Royal Academy. During his lifetime he was a very popular artist and had little difficulty in selling his charming, though sentimental, watercolours. This example, showing a cottage bedecked with climbers, is typical of his work, with every effort taken to make the flowers recognizable.

At the opposite extreme from Strachan's meticulous detail is the rapid, sketching quality of Theresa Stannard's depiction of flowers. Stannard (1898–1947) was the only daughter of Henry John Sylvester Stannard. Her father taught her how to paint and draw, and at an early age she was a proficient artist. In 1909 Queen Alexandra bought one of her watercolours, and in 1915 at the age of 16 she became the youngest ever exhibitor at the Royal Academy. In 1923 she held a joint exhibition with her father at the Brook Street Gallery where Queen Mary bought one of her garden scenes. Her reputation spread throughout England in the inter-War years, and the royal family continued to buy her watercolours; one which they purchased in 1931 for £21 was described by the King as a 'delightful scheme of colour'.

Not everyone was so complimentary, however; one reviewer in the *Birmingham Post* (6 March 1928) wrote: 'in colour [the garden pictures] are fresh and clear, and in handling they are confident and capable, but they do lack something of the largeness of vision which is required in dealing with garden subjects if the suspicion of fussiness is to be avoided and the restfulness of the well arranged garden is to be suggested. That Miss Stannard is a devout and careful student of nature is not to be questioned but she still has something to learn about the value of elimination in picture making.'

AT THE COTTAGE DOOR
David Woodlock

Thomas Mackay's charming and delicate watercolours are different in technique from those of his contemporaries, largely for the way that watercolour is used to create an impression through the use of stippled effects, as can be seen in this delightful example of his work. He was born in Morpeth and seems to have spent much of his time in Warwickshire, when not working as an architect in Newcastle. He is known to have been active as a painter between 1878 and 1905, having only taken it up at the relatively late age of twenty-seven.

David Woodlock's garden watercolours are also very different from those of his contemporaries and his style is immediately identifiable. He was not interested in carefully delineating flowers and gardens, but wanted to give a broader impression of what he saw. The success of his technique lay in his application of watercolour to wet paper, fusing the colours together. The result, as here, is altogether hazier and less defined than conventional garden painting, but conveys the image of a garden burgeoning with plants, and indifferent to 'design'. He was born in Southern Ireland in County Tipperary in 1842. When he came to England he studied art in Liverpool and painted in both oil and watercolour. He became a member of the Liverpool Academy and was a founder of the Liverpool Sketching Club. From 1880 he exhibited at the principal London galleries and at the Royal Academy and the Royal Institute for Painters in Watercolour. He died in 1929.

GIRL AND DUCKS BEFORE A WATERMILL
Thomas Mackay

OUTSIDE THE COTTAGE
Arthur Claude Strachan

GIRL AND CAT OUTSIDE COTTAGE
Arthur Claude Strachan

The image of the cottage garden, in the hands of Strachan, Woodlock, and the younger Stannards, was far removed from the image offered by Birket Foster and Helen Allingham. Richly floriferous, cleansed of any but the aesthetically pleasing trappings of poverty, with little or nothing of the kitchen about it, this Edwardian image served to idealize the cottager's life in a period not yet recovered from agricultural depression, and to promote an increasingly fashionable style of planting.

Remembering Richard Jefferies' accusation, in *Amaryllis at the Fair*, about the idealization of the countryside in popular painting – 'Touched up designs; a tree taken from one place, a brook from another, a house from another – *and mixed to order*, like a prescription by the chemist – xv.grs. grass, 3 dr. stile, iiij, grs. rustic bridge' – one could characterize an immense number of cottage scenes in the 1890s and Edwardian period as one part each of stocks, delphiniums, hollyhocks, sunflowers, rocket, carnations, poppies, pansies, and clematis; three parts thatch, one part half-timbering, and one woman with apron to still any doubts about the social status of the occupants. At least these pictures of Strachan's, with potted pelargoniums on the windowsill in one case and what appear to be bean-stakes in the other, contain a few reminders that cottage gardens were not solely demonstration grounds for the 'old-fashioned' flowers in vogue in the last years of the Victorian period.

HOLMWOOD, SURREY
Alberto Pisa

We have seen that the distinction between the labourer's cottage and the middle-class small house was already effaced, as far as gardening literature was concerned, by the 1880s. During the Edwardian period the situation was to become even more confused, as the process of gentrification began to sweep through the rural villages – at least in the southern counties. M. R. Gloag complained in her *Book of English Gardens* (1906) that: 'To define a Cottage Garden is difficult, especially now that the present-day craze for spending week-ends in the country has resulted in many

an old Cottage and Garden passing out of the villagers' hands into the possession of a very different class, to be adapted, changed, and added to by their new owners; the one thing remaining unchanged being their name. It may appear a dogmatic statement, but experience seems to show that a true Cottage Garden can only be created by a villager. Of course they have been imitated, but in the imitation a strange under-current of educated taste peeps out that spoils in the copy the character of the original; much of the charm of which lies in the simple combination of flowers and vegetables

that only a cottager can produce.'

The process of gentrification is reflected in Alberto Pisa's portrayal of the garden at Holmwood – his home from 1913. Charles Thonger specifically said that his *Book of the Cottage Garden* (1909) 'is written for those who, whilst possessing country cottages, are in no sense cottagers. Nowadays "a cottage in the country" may mean anything from a six-roomed bungalow with a diminutive garden to a commodious residence surrounded by extensive grounds.' Certainly the garden in Stannard's picture seems larger than that of a 'real' cottage.

A Cottage Garden

Theresa Stannard

MOTHER AND CHILD OUTSIDE SMALL HOUSES
Thomas Nicholson Tyndale

VILLAGE SCENE
Thomas Mackay

The provision of gardens for workers' housing had been a cause earnestly promoted by the reformers of the early Victorian period, and put into practice at model industrial communities like Saltaire near Bradford and philanthropic settlements like Talbot Village near Bournemouth. By the end of the century, with the idea of the Garden City in the air, model villages were being created for a wide social spectrum, from the middle-class Webb Estate at Purley, Surrey, where private houses were fitted into a pre-arranged landscape and maintenance of the gardens was made a condition of leasehold, to the proposals of A.C. Sennett for workers' horticultural societies as part of the social basis of every garden city. The hedged enclosure in front of the cottage (to be seen both left and right), often filled with roses or old-fashioned plants, was coming to be a customary appendage for housing estates, especially if they followed vernacular modes of architecture.

Increasingly, as villages became gentrified, they were brought into line with the picturesque image of rural life as presented by the cottage garden painters. The villages of the Thames valley, for example, were promoted in the early years of this century by such devices as ornamental gardening on the canal banks and by the garden of John Fothergill's pub at Thame, the Spread Eagle.

GIRL WITH KITTEN OUTSIDE A HOUSE
Arthur Claude Strachan

WOMAN BEFORE A COTTAGE
Arthur Claude Strachan

The Edwardian period saw not only middle-class cottages, model villages and garden cities; it also saw the beginning of complaints about the decline of the cottage garden. George Bourne reported the following accusation by an Edwardian landowner: 'The men, he said, holding their cottages as one of the conditions of employment on the farms, had grown idle, and were neglecting the cottage gardens – were neglecting them so seriously that, in the interests of the estate, he had been obliged to complain to the farmers. Upon my asking for explanations of a disposition so unlike that of the labourers in this parish, many of whom were not content with their cottage gardens, but take more ground when they can get it, my friend said deliberately: "I think food is too cheap. With their fifteen shillings a week the men can buy all they want without working for it; and the result is that they waste their evenings and the gardens go to ruin."'

Bourne's own explanation of the alleged decline was the increase in tenancy as against ownership: cottagers who owned their own houses had gardens that were well kept, while those who rented by the week neglected theirs. However, a similar complaint was voiced by Mrs Davidson, writing in E. T. Cook's *Gardens of England* (1908): '... the best-kept gardens belong most frequently to elderly people. The younger and stronger members of village communities spend their scanty leisure mostly in other ways than in tilling to the best advantage the plot of ground which seldom fails to fall to their share.' One such distraction may have been the growing popularity of the cinema, which was blamed for dwindling attendances at provincial flower shows before the First World War.

Neglected and meagre cottage gardens, however, while they played their part in the pictures of Birket Foster and Allingham at the beginning of the cottage-garden cult, were played down by their successors in the early twentieth century. Artists like Strachan continued to portray cottage gardens in high keeping, like that shown above with its masses of hollyhocks, poppies, asters and phlox: whatever the social reality of the cottage garden, the horticultural image had become fixed in the public mind.

PERGOLA
Lilian Stannard

CHAPTER III

THE COUNTRY HOUSE GARDEN

THE great country estate of mid-Victorian times was in some ways less like a suburban family garden than like a business corporation; it was managed by a large staff with a well-defined hierarchy of skills and responsibilities, ranging from apprentices through the foremen of different departments (pleasure ground, glass) to the head gardener. Some gardens were well known as training centres adding lustre to a curriculum vitae; there was much competition for successful head gardeners to move on to progressively better-known estates. The gardener's skills were tested not only by the management of the kitchen garden, much of which by mid-century was under glass to ensure year-round cropping, by the appearance of the ornamental gardens, and by the production and arrangement of floral displays for the dinner-table, but also by a system of flower shows and competitions, regional and national, at which he could measure his abilities against those of his peers on other estates. Gardening in the second half of the nineteenth century was a skilled profession, and the major gardeners could become virtually national figures; Joseph Paxton had gone so far as to win a knighthood and enter Parliament.

The gardener was expected to be skilled in botany and art as well as practical gardening. New plant species were continually arriving from abroad; the gardener had to work out their requirements and optimum growing conditions by practical experiment, and then determine the best ways of using them in the garden. In this task he was given a free hand by the newly ascendant taste of the Victorian period. The generation of the 1820s and 1830s reacted sharply against the English landscape garden, which had been dominant for the best part of a century, and had held up the ideal of the imitation of nature; the writings of John Claudius Loudon (1783–1843), the leading writer on gardening of his period, spread the contrary gospel of the rejection of nature and of the garden as a work of art. Loudon condemned as in bad taste the attempt to deceive the spectator into thinking that what he saw was the work of unaided nature. The garden was a work of art, and must be seen to be a work of art; and that required a deliberate artifice, making the hand of man apparent at every turn. There were two ways of making a garden a work of art, he declared: giving it a formal design, or planting it with exotic plants that could not be confused with the native flora; and under his influence, the flower garden and the collection of exotic trees, most notably of conifers, became the centre of attention in the ornamental garden.

It is the flower garden that most concerns us here. From being a hidden feature in the eighteenth century, screened from the principal views by shrubberies so that it did not interfere with the 'natural' image of the landscape, it had become the most prominent item in the view by mid-nineteenth century. Gardeners soon discovered that the new exotics – especially the half-hardy perennials, like pelargoniums, verbenas, and calceolarias, that had to be protected under glass during the English winters but could flourish outdoors during the summer months – gave them the opportunity to change the appearance of the flower garden every year, and eventually every season. By the 1840s the rules of the 'bedding system' were being worked out. The first principle was 'massing', as distinguished from what was looked back on as the indiscriminate mixing of flowers in the previous generation: each bed was to be filled with one type of flower only, for the most emphatic effect of colour. Colours were to be arranged for high contrast: adjacent beds should be widely separated on the spectrum. The habits of the plants used should balance each other as well as their colours. As book after book on the theory of colour was published in the 1840s and 1850s, their merits were debated in the gardening press, and gardeners put their propositions to practical test in the flower garden. It has been popular in recent years to credit Gertrude Jekyll with an unprecedented role in introducing the values of art into the flower garden, but the books she studied in art school were precisely those the head gardeners of her youth were using to guide their experiments in bedding.

Formal bedding occupied the primary position in the flower garden – the main focus of the view from the house. But other parts of the garden allowed for other sorts of experiment: mixed or herbaceous borders, which used a range of plants for which this sort of massing was unsuitable, were the object of much attention, although Donald Beaton (whose weekly column in *The Cottage Gardener* during the 1850s was a major influence on the period) was disappointed in the lack of progress the mixed border seemed to be making. He regarded it as the great unsolved problem of garden art.

By the 1860s, the values of the bedding system were firmly established, and many younger gardeners were looking for new and opposed ideas – the use of foliage rather than flowers, playing down the high contrasts of colour, returning to a mixture of flowers within the bed. The values of this generation were summed up in *The English Flower Garden* (1883), an anthology of the writings of the major gardeners of the period, edited by the acerbic gardening journalist William Robinson. In it he gave prominence to the view of William Wildsmith, gardener at Heckfield Place, Hampshire, that what was

known as colour planning ought to be avoided altogether: 'the various colours should be so completely commingled that one would be puzzled to determine what tint predominates in the entire arrangement ... if any colour at all may predominate, it is what gardeners know as "glaucous," that is, a light grey or whitish green.' The less radical still agreed that contrast was undesirable, and that a single colour ought to dominate the flower garden. Ideas on harmony had reversed themselves since the Beaton years; then it had been accepted that colours only harmonized when they were separated in the spectrum, but in *The English Flower Garden* it was argued that colours harmonized only when adjacent, like red and orange, or orange and yellow.

These ideas were to be challenged in their turn by Gertrude Jekyll, who revived the emphasis on colour theory characteristic of mid-century – though in her case it was the border rather than the bedding scheme on the parterre that formed the setting for colour experiments. The graded sequence of colours as the eye moved down the border, cool at either end and warm, sometimes brilliant, in the middle, became widely popular during the Edwardian period. Jekyll also tamed the idea of the one-colour garden. 'It is a curious thing', she wrote, 'that people will sometimes spoil some garden project for the sake of a word', and she recommended setting off the dominant colour with complementary colours – e.g. touches of yellow in a blue garden.

As these changes in style became more widespread, they were accompanied by a demand in some quarters for a change in the role of the gardener. As early as the 1870s voices were raised against his dominance on the estate. 'Have you no proper spirit left, that you submit to be dictated to by a servant?' demanded the popular writer John Latouche in his *Country House Essays*, but this was to misconceive the role of a skilled professional on a country estate. It was particularly the middle classes who responded to this denigration of the gardener, and who warmed to the idea of his replacement by unskilled labourers, who would merely follow orders.

By the turn of the century a new type of garden writing was emerging, based on the smaller house, and emphasizing the garden as an expression of the owner's personality. The writings of Alfred Austin (*The Garden that I Love*, 1894), Gertrude Jekyll (*Wood and Garden*, 1899; *Home and Garden*, 1900), Walter P. Wright (*The Perfect Garden*, 1911; *The New Gardening*, 1912), and Marion Cran (*The Garden of Ignorance*, 1913) represented the owner as the artistic force in the garden. Wright was explicit in removing the gardener from any central role: 'People who take plants into their lives should never be content to let alien hands arrange them, any more than they should permit their drawing-rooms to be finished off by the decorators. Outside help must come in, it is true. The shovelling out of earth, the beating down of turf, the wheeling of manure, are as obviously the tasks of hired labour as the papering of walls and the laying of carpets. But beyond this there should be nothing done in which the hand of the owner is not prominent.' Gardeners seldom appear in the paintings included in this volume; the image of the garden promoted by these painters had little room for labour, or indeed for the practical necessities of garden maintenance. A further passage from Wright suggests the disparity between the painted image and the reality that the homeowner found when trying to create a Beatrice Parsons scene in his own garden: 'The trouble lies in the difficulty which people have in harmonising the practical with the ideal. In the garden, as in the human being, they see certain characteristics which appeal to their best instincts. The beauty of a rose garden stimulates them like the eloquence of a statesman. They find the same intellectual pleasure in a good herbaceous border as in the performance of a great actor. But they find it as difficult to imagine that the rose garden is built on ordure as to comprehend that the cabinet minister has climbed upwards by devious paths of party strategy ...'

AN AMATEUR
Frederick Walker

Representations of work in the kitchen garden are rare in Victorian painting, and the example shown here depicts not the garden staff at work, but as the title – 'An Amateur' or 'Coachman and Cabbage' – indicates, an interloper from another department of the household about to help himself to an impromptu harvest.

Frederick Walker was born in Marylebone in 1840, the son of an amateur artist who encouraged his artistic leanings. After spending some time with an architect his talent became apparent and he was admitted as a student to the Royal Academy Schools. He was also a member of the Langham Sketching Club. To earn a living he started doing book illustrations with other artists such as J. W. North and G. J. Pinwell. He first exhibited at the Royal Academy in 1863 and the Old Watercolour Society in 1864. For health reasons he travelled to Algiers in 1873–4 and died in 1875. He was buried in his favourite sketching ground at Cookham on Thames.

Walker was strongly influenced by the Pre-Raphaelites, and this can be seen both in his palette and in his minute and detailed representation of nature. But unlike the Pre-Raphaelites, Walker was also interested in portraying people behaving naturally in their own environment. Van Gogh admired Walker's work and wrote in a letter of 1885, 'they [Walker and Pinwell] did in England what Maris, Israels, Mauve have done in Holland, namely restored nature over convention; sentiment and impression over academic platitudes and dullness ... They were the first tonists.'

GARDEN SCENE
Beatrice Parsons

THE WALLED GARDEN
Arthur Foord Hughes

Pictures of the kitchen garden tended not only to eliminate the spectacle of the working gardener, but also to concentrate on one particular style of kitchen garden – the floral. Whether flowers had any place in the kitchen garden, or whether it should be purely functional, was a subject for debate throughout the Victorian period; some critics argued that uniform rows of cabbages, carrots and the like were sufficiently beautiful in themselves not to require floral ornamentation. Many country house owners, however, liked to have a floriferous kitchen garden as a place to show their guests, and some head gardeners, whose houses were in many cases part of the kitchen garden itself, treated it as their own private flower garden. A prominent gardener like Peter Grieve of Culford Hall, Suffolk, for instance, re-designed his kitchen garden so that a formal avenue of flower beds and yew hedges led to the door of his own house – a fitting sign of the importance of his position. By the Edwardian period, however, the commercial availability of fresh produce was changing some kitchen-garden habits, and the process of turning some of them from functional into purely ornamental gardens was already beginning.

The presence of daffodils among the tulips and irises in the picture on the left identifies it as dating from the 1880s, for until that period daffodils had not been widely popular. In that decade the great bulb merchant Peter Barr began a campaign to rediscover all the daffodil varieties ever grown in England, and their popularity began to increase. Note also the presence of bee-boles in the watercolour above: a sign that what might otherwise seem merely a walled flower garden had in fact begun as a kitchen garden.

THE GARDEN PATH
Beatrice Parsons

Victorian gardens, large and small, made great use of plants kept in tubs and pots. One reason for this fascination was their artificiality – a quality highly important to a generation in rebellion against a standardized conception of nature. Growing in pots 'always checks and counteracts the natural habits of the plant', as Loudon observed, and therefore provided a challenge for the gardener. Loudon recommended as an example a garden where the tree collection was kept in tubs, and was therefore movable. Greenhouses and conservatories remained essentially collections of plants in pots until the 1870s, when ideas of interior landscape came in. For the smaller garden, there were the three editions, beginning in the 1820s, of *Flora Domestica*, a manual on potted plants by Elizabeth Kent, sister-in-law of the poet Leigh Hunt.

Noel Smith's picture shows tubbed agapanthus alternated with the clipped trees; in Parsons' picture, we see a much more common device – vases of pelargoniums capping the pilasters of a garden wall, an effect much used in Victorian times to give a red hue to the distance. Nearer the house, tubbed pelargoniums could be put to much greater use; in the 1860s it became fashionable to train them into pyramidal shape, and 'geranium pyramids' – consisting of cones of rubble with potted pelargoniums plunged in to produce floral cones well over human height – experienced a brief period of glory.

THE COURT GARDEN, HINTON
Noel Smith

THE ROSE GARDEN
Charles Edward Wilson

THE ROSES
Beatrice Parsons

One department of the garden which continued throughout Victorian times to be secluded from the principal view was the rose garden. Long after the other flowers had been brought into the foreground, roses continued to be segregated from the rest of the garden; for one thing, they were uninteresting to look at for much of the year. A further reason was that the hues of the roses available during the Victorian period did not readily conform to the requirements of High Victorian colour theory. Victorian roses were predominantly white, pink,

crimson, purplish, and, from the middle of the century, yellow – not bright enough to meet the requirements of the main display as laid down by the doyens of the bedding system. It was not until after the turn of the century that rose breeding began to produce bright scarlet and orange tints; and this development was paralleled by the appearance of rose beds in the parterre in front of the house. The Victorian rose garden, whether formally or informally laid out, had been placed away from the main views, as it is in Beatrice Parsons picture, and

screened by shrubberies or hedges.

A partial exception to this rule was the use of roses pruned as standards, a technique introduced from France which became popular from the 1820s onwards. Standard roses could be used for lining the smaller avenues or to give vertical scale to a group of flower beds, creating variety and contrast in an otherwise uniform display. Note too how carefully Wilson has matched the colour of the pink and yellow roses in the lady's basket to the bloom in her cheeks and the colour of her sash.

WHITE LILIES
Lilian Stannard

New trends in the use of roses began to make themselves felt during the last quarter of the century. In particular, there was increased interest in growing roses in a free, natural manner rather than in the carefully trained way generally adopted hitherto: vigorous shrubs, for example, or the training of climbing roses through trees or hedges were popular methods. The depiction of the roses in Johnson's picture exemplifies this and shows just how far some gardeners had already gone by 1877, although this use of roses became an important theme in the writings of Gertrude Jekyll after the turn of the century. Edward Killingworth Johnson (1825–96), born in Stratford-le-Bow, became a full-time painter in 1863. His work is often highly detailed and Pre-Raphaelite in manner as the delicate rendering of the brocading of his subject's skirt and of the roses shows.

Lilian Stannard (1877–1944) was one of the most talented of the garden artists working at the turn of the century. She was born at Foxfield. the daughter of Henry Stannard, and sister of H. J. Sylvester Stannard. By the age of thirty she had become one of the best-known painters of flowers and gardens in England and many of her pictures were reproduced in gardening books. The white of the lilies and the sunlit borders are here magnificently contrasted with the dark green of the shaded arbour, while the pansies and the sweet william provide a splash of warm colour. In 1899 the *Bedfordshire Times* described one of her pictures as 'of such minute fidelity as to bear strutiny with a magnifier. This lady's exact drawing and colouring should be of great value to publishers and men of science, but there is also poetry in the notion and composition.'

THE ROSE BOWER
Edward Killingworth Johnson

PICKING FLOWERS
Arthur Hopkins

THE SPINNING WHEEL
David Woodlock

Arthur Hopkins (1848–1930) was the brother of the poet Gerard Manley Hopkins. He worked for twenty-five years as an illustrator for *Graphic* and *Punch*; his pictures can range from superb to rather laboured imitations of his contemporaries. 'Picking Flowers' is a magnificent example of his work and the fresh colours and fluid watercolour technique are almost impressionist in their vibrancy.

The delicate lilac flowers the lady is picking are, of course, clematis. Until the nineteenth century only the native European and American species were widely grown; Asiatic species replaced these in popularity, especially after the introduction of *C. montana* in the 1830s, and attempts at hybridization were begun. George Jackman produced his first important hybrid, *Clematis × jackmanii*, in 1862 at his Woking nursery, and by the time of the publication of his monograph *Clematis as a Garden Flower* (1872), he could list more than 200 species and varieties: 'Thus, within the last ten years, the Hardy Clematis has been converted from an ordinary climbing shrub, handsome indeed in some, and elegant in all its forms, to one of the most gorgeous of gardening ornaments, unrivalled as a flowering woody climber . . .'. He promoted the use of clematis for pot culture, bedding (pegged down to cover the soil), training as pillars and pyramids, trailing in the rock garden, and of course as the centre of attention in special clematis gardens or climberies.

SPRING
Beatrice Parsons

By far the most important arboreal fashion during the Victorian period was the preference for conifers, a taste which has led to the predominance in gardens of cypresses, monkey-puzzles and redwoods. Part of their attraction was their evergreen quality, giving interest to the garden even in the depths of winter. The need to fill this seasonal gap also in part underlay the fashion for evergreens such as hollies, rhododendrons and magnolias, all of which were extensively hybridized – though the latter two were more important for their flowers than for their foliage. Although North American magnolias had been introduced and become popular during the eighteenth century, it was the arrival in the early nineteenth century of Chinese species that led to the creation of the foremost hydrid range – *Magnolia* × *soulangiana*, first raised in France and almost certainly the one shown here. In 1829 Young of Epsom bought up the entire stock of the hybrid and began distributing it in England.

By the last quarter of the century a reaction was setting in against the dominance of the evergreen, whether promoted by the partisans of native British trees, like the architect Reginald Blomfield, by the enthusiasts of the wild garden, who wanted trees that could be underplanted with spring flowers, or by nurserymen like William Paul, who from the 1870s was calling for more colour planning in the wider landscape and the massed planting of flowering trees and trees with coloured leaves or bark. All these interests converged by the turn of the century in the creation of scenes like the above, with laburnum, horse chestnuts, rhododendrons, and hawthorns creating a variety of colour and foliage.

A QUIET PLACE
Beatrice Parsons

A SUMMER'S AFTERNOON
Henry John Sylvester Stannard

Two contrasting approaches to the flower garden are illustrated here. The central tradition of Victorian gardening – the formal parterre – is represented by Stannard's water-colour shown above, but even here it has altered considerably from its High Victorian days. The colour schemes of the 1840s to 1870s, based on high contrast, have been replaced by the late Victorian preference for a narrow colour range, in this case carried out in pelargoniums and alyssum. Whereas in the 1840s it was felt that colours only harmonized if they were widely separated in the spectrum – red

and blue, for instance – by the 1880s it was coming to be felt that colours only harmonized when adjacent in the spectrum – e.g. red and orange. This taste found its fullest expression in the one-colour garden.

On the right is a mixed border, a form of gardening which posed great problems for the High Victorians because the height and form of the herbaceous plants rendered them unsuitable for the carefully balanced masses of colour which contemporary colour theory prescribed. 'Mixed borders we all have, or ought to have', wrote Donald Beaton in the 1850s, but 'I never

yet saw even a good or tolerable disposition of such plants anywhere.' By the 1870s taste was changing, and such borders were coming to be admired for their very freedom from colour schemes: as Shirley Hibberd said, in the herbaceous border incidents were everything and symmetry nothing. This idea obviously appealed to the artist Harry E. James, who was mainly a landscape and coastal painter, and only sometimes turned to garden scenes. He exhibited regularly between 1882 and 1912, and spent much of his working life in the West Country, mainly in Cornwall and Devon.

HERBACEOUS BORDER
Harry E. James

OLD-WORLD GARDEN
Harry E. James

The planning of mixed borders was given new impetus from the 1880s by Gertrude Jekyll. Not only did she popularize the grouping of plants in informal, naturalistic drifts instead of blocks and lines, but she encouraged the treating of the border as an integrated sequence of colours, moving from cold colours at either end through to a series of warmer, often quite intense, colours in the middle. Something of this graded colour sequence can be seen in Lilian Stannard's picture, in the progression from pansies and irises to poppies, asters, delphiniums, lilies, and heleniums. The picture by James allows us to see the process of staking and tying needed to maintain the taller plants of the border and intermingled climbing plants, such as the climbing roses shown here, in upright condition.

Lilian Stannard's career as a painter blossomed during the years when Jekyll's reputation became firmly established. Among her admirers was the Princess of Wales, who bought one of her pictures from her 'one-man' exhibition at the Mendoza Gallery. Commenting on Stannard's work displayed at this exhibition a reviewer wrote in *The Observer* (29 April 1906): 'I defy any lover of an old-fashioned English garden to see these drawings without real delight. There is a peace, a repose, almost a fragrance about each and all of them. Take "The Rosery, Stagsden Vicarage": look at the unlaboured way in which the beautiful result is reached; turn anywhere, and see the foxgloves, the delphiniums, the stately hollyhocks, the tender greens, the sunny atmosphere, and then you will not wonder that men will struggle for forty years in any part of the world so as to come home at last and die in a house set in an old English garden.'

THE GARDEN PATH
Lilian Stannard

LAVINGTON, SUSSEX
James Matthews

ROBIN IN A GARDEN
Beatrice Parsons

By the beginning of the twentieth century, under the influence of Gertrude Jekyll, the great debates on colour planning that had characterized the High Victorian period had returned, although most gardeners were unaware of the extent to which they were invoking principles familiar to their predecessors. 'Flower-grouping for colour is almost a new study in gardens', wrote Walter P. Wright in his *Perfect Garden* (1911). 'The first study in flower-gardening should be Colour – not System, not Design, but Colour. System and Design separate gardeners, Colour unites them.' The colour taste of the period was returning, as in the 1840s and 1850s, to brilliance. 'Why do our park gardeners persist in the subordination of warm brilliant colours to cold tints – yellows and greens?' asked a critic in the *Journal of Horticulture* in 1909. As reds and scarlets returned to favour in the hierarchy of colours, greater emphasis was also accorded to arches, pergolas, and pillars, to give vertical scale by hoisting clematis, climbing roses, and the new hybrid sweet peas into prominent positions as in the picture above.

The picture by James Matthews shows an Edwardian flower garden for the smaller house – typical rather than exemplary, though the balancing of tall hollyhocks by pillar roses is in the spirit of the new gardening of the period. Very little is known about the artist, except that he worked in Sussex at the end of the nineteenth century and that he was influenced by Helen Allingham; nonetheless, his almost schematic rendering of the flowers makes many of them virtually unidentifiable.

WORKERS IN A FIELD
William Harford

William Harford's picture gives us a rare glimpse of the more commercial side of the garden: here, fields of lavender are being harvested. Lavender was grown extensively in northern Surrey, around the area of Mitcham, during the later nineteenth century. A department of the garden which increased in importance in the late Victorian period was the reserve garden – the area in which flowers were grown for cutting. Preparing floral settings for the dining table had become one of the gardener's duties by the 1870s, and around the turn of the century cut flowers began to succeed foliage plants for indoor decoration (foliage plants had proved hardier under gaslight). Some gardens, like Bloxholm Hall in Lincolnshire, were maintained primarily to provide flowers for decorating the owner's London house, a feat made possible in the nineteenth century by the development of the railways.

Mildred Anne Butler was born in Kilmarry, County Kilkenny, in 1858, the daughter of Captain Henry Butler, an amateur artist whose work influenced his daughter. Her watercolours were very popular during her lifetime and for forty years she was a regular exhibitor at the Royal Academy, the Old Watercolour Society, and the Royal Hibernian Academy. In 1893 her work was included in an album given by the Society of Lady Artists to Princess Mary on her marriage to the Duke of York; Queen Mary later acquired two more of her works, one of them a small watercolour for the Queen's Doll's House at Windsor.

Many of her watercolours depicted gardens – 'a tribute to William Robinson's dramatic innovations in design'. Her free, often impressionistic style was well-suited to catching the dramatic impact of a mass of flowers.

COLLECTING FLOWERS
Mildred Anne Butler

THE YOUNG GARDENERS
Mary Hayllar

THE LITTLE GARDENER
Harold Swanwick

The little girls in Mary Hayllar's picture are obviously the gardener's daughters, helping their father carry the azaleas; the girl in Harold Swanwick's watercolour is equally clearly the daughter of the house. 'The union of home and garden is a sacred social duty', wrote Walter P. Wright in *The Perfect Garden* (1911). 'The garden-home is the seat of the purest affections, the truest outlook on life, the highest conception of humanity.' But the garden-home was something very different from the traditional country house garden, administered by a specially trained staff. 'People who take plants into their lives should never be content to let alien hands arrange them', advised Wright; 'there should be nothing done in which the hand of the owner is not prominent'. The home-owner, not the gardener, was the important figure in the creation of the dream garden of the Edwardian period; these two watercolours illustrate one of the turning-points in this conception of the garden.

Mary Hayllar was the youngest and least well-known member of a family of talented artists. While her father and sisters achieved considerable esteem in the art world, Mary's career was confined to a few years in the early 1880s, and ceased when she married. Harold Swanwick (1866–1929) was born in Middlesex; few biographical details are known about his life except that he studied in Liverpool and at the Slade and exhibited at the Royal Academy from 1889.

PICKING FLOWERS
Helen Allingham

CHAPTER IV

THE WILD GARDEN

 HE wild garden is a concept associated today primarily with William Robinson (1838–1935), who coined the term. In the hundred or so years since his book, *The Wild Garden*, first appeared in 1870, the phrase has been given a variety of meanings, and as early as the 1881 edition of his book Robinson was forced to distinguish his meaning from its rivals: 'It has nothing to do with the old idea of the "Wilderness." It does not mean the picturesque garden, for a garden may be highly picturesque, and yet in every part the result of ceaseless care ... Some have thought of it as a garden run wild, or sowing annuals in a muddle; whereas it does not interfere with the regulation flower garden at all. I wish it to be kept distinctly in the mind from the various sorts of hardy plant cultivation in groups, beds, and borders ... distinct from the rock garden ... from the ordinary type of "Spring Garden;" and from our own beautiful native flowers ...' Robinson's idea lay in 'placing plants of other countries, as hardy as our hardiest wild flowers, in places where they will flourish *without further care or cost*'. Low maintenance, and the naturalization of exotics, were the two themes of his wild garden: 'naturalizing or making wild innumerable beautiful natives of many regions of the earth in our woods, wild and semi-wild places, rougher parts of pleasure grounds, etc., and in unoccupied places in almost every kind of garden.' It was envisaged as a supplement to, not a replacement of, traditional ways of gardening, and especially as a way of beautifying the outlying portions of an estate. The wild garden scenes illustrated by Alfred Parsons in the 1894 edition of Robinson's book were for the most part on estates which also boasted grand formal gardens with the full panoply of bedding and artifice.

Robinson's arguments for the merits of wild gardening laid stress on the reduction of maintenance involved. Since there was no formal element, no disagreeable effects would result from plants dying or decaying in situ. Particular stress was laid on plants that would become rampant: Robinson praised comfrey, for instance, because it would 'soon run about, exterminate the weeds, and prove quite a lesson in wild and natural gardening'. He remained opposed to an indiscriminate variety of specimens, consistently urging a broad effect in planting: 'The chief rule should be – never show the naked earth: carpet or clothe it with dwarf subjects, and then allow the taller ones to rise in their own wild way through the turf or spray.' This demand for massed

planting could create moral difficulties, however. A forester wrote to Robinson's magazine *The Garden* in 1876, telling how he had transplanted three cartloads each of daffodils and lilies of the valley to improve his woods; another correspondent in reply protested against such wholescale plundering: 'there is something selfish in wholesale cartloading away of the flowers of our meadows, banks, hedges, and copses, and ... if encouraged it will certainly endanger not the wild gardens but the woodlands'.

This, then, was Robinson's idea of the wild garden – in practice, not a concept original with him, for prominent gardens like Cliveden and Elvaston Castle already existed to be pointed to as examples, and the naturalization of bulbs in grass can be traced back to the first half of the nineteenth century as a gardening technique. Robinson was nonetheless the major popularizer of the idea, and it rapidly became identified with him.

However, he could not control the copyright of his phrase, and it had soon come to mean a variety of other things. In particular, it had come to mean a garden that gave a visual impression of wildness, even if at the expense of great labour. Many of the horticultural fashions of the 1880s and 1890s depended on the relaxation of an earlier love of precision and symmetry. Camellias with large, floppy flowers supplanted the varieties with tightly geometrical flowers that the High Victorians had loved; taste in roses turned to bushy shrubs and climbers that could be trained to grow up trees and through hedges; William Wildsmith of Heckfield Place in Hampshire pioneered deliberately ragged and disorderly forms of bedding in which the planting trailed over the edge of the bed and herbaceous plants competed with each other instead of being neatly staked and tied. The quest for effects of deliberate wildness fitted comfortably with this aesthetic.

The major problem of the wild garden in the nineteenth century was the extent to which it was supposed to be an imitation of nature. Should one imitate specific bits of natural scenery, or follow a general principle? should one mass plants on a large scale, or scatter them as individuals? The answer depended in large part on what one meant by nature. Was nature disorderly? S.W. Fitzherbert in his *Book of the Wild Garden* (1903), thought not; 'there is no sign of disorder in a thoughtfully planned and planted example' of wild gardening, he wrote, any more than in genuine Nature: 'It is when Nature reasserts her sway in spots which man has ceased to cultivate that the tangle of brambles and nettles merits the term "disorder".' Walter P. Wright, on the other hand, in his book *The Perfect Garden* (1911), argued in post-Darwinian terms that nature was a bad guide to follow: 'Nature is not the truest guide to artistic gardening. She is sometimes forcible, but she is invariably crude. She uses flowers, as she uses tragedies, without any thought for effect. Her

work is merely the outcome of the instincts of reproduction, and of killing... Nature flings plants about very much as she flings blows. They grow where the conditions suit them. It may be that they have a beauty of their own, but it is not the beauty of educated thought. The flowers are not there to express ideals of beauty; they are there for increase.'

Those architects who promoted the formal garden – men like Reginald Blomfield and J.D. Sedding – enthusiastically encouraged the growing of native flowers, but were neutral or dismissive about the claims of wildness in design. But the final word, including an acknowledgement of the role of the artist in popularizing the image of the wild garden, can be left to the landscape gardener George Abbey, writing in the *Journal of Horticulture* in 1909 of facsimile imitations of natural scenery: 'This cannot be considered as belonging to gardening as an art of culture, because in them all appearance of culture is to be avoided; and they cannot be considered as belonging to the gardening as a fine art, because it is not intended that the result shall be recognized as the work of art, but it shall be mistaken for Nature itself; in short, that the spectator should be imposed upon. Such gardens – that is to say, the present time wild garden, for instance – do not require to be made by gardeners; any person possessing a painter's eye, and assisted by country labourers ... will form them just as well as a landscape gardener.'

GIRLS PICKING FLOWERS
Carlton Alfred Smith

ROSES
Helen Allingham

'A taste for Natural history', said Loudon in his *Magazine of Natural History*, 'is superior, in a social point of view, even to a taste for gardening.' Natural history indeed became both a popular amusement and a staple part of popular education during the Victorian period. Botanical rambles were a standard part of the well-bred young woman's experience, and some gardening fashions such as the craze for ferns were largely sustained by women. Charles Kingsley recommended fern collecting for young ladies as a more beneficial occupation than Berlin wool-work, and his daughter Char-

lotte Chanter published a volume entitled *Ferny Combes* (1856) about her rambles hunting for ferns in Devonshire. The cornflowers, irises, dog daisies, poppies and wild roses of these two pictures were all likely targets for such expeditions.

Carlton Alfred Smith (1853–1946) was born in London. His artistic talents were encouraged from an early age by his father (a steel engraver); he was educated in France and later studied at the Slade. After leaving the Slade he became a lithographer and it was only later that he could afford to become a full-time

painter. He started exhibiting from 1879, mainly at the Royal Society of British Artists and the Royal Institute of Painters in Water-colour. to which he was elected a member in 1889. Like many watercolourists working at the end of the nineteenth century, he had a fascination for detail and meticulously recorded it. He is perhaps best remembered for his genre pictures, particularly those showing women in a domestic interior. Here the women are brought into the open where the artist demonstrates his skill in conveying intensity of colour and subtle effects of light.

SPRING, ISLE OF WIGHT
Beatrice Parsons

In the early days of the bedding system, its advocates had argued for the practice of devoting large beds to one variety of flower by drawing an analogy with nature 'who in a wild state scatters profusely en masse', as a contributor to the *Gardener's Magazine* put it in 1828. Such arguments were revived in the 1860s and 1870s as massing came under attack; D.T. Fish wrote in the *Gardeners' Chronicle* in 1868: 'Colour is one of our richest heritages . . . and

lest we should overlook it, Nature has spread abroad masses of it by the mile . . . in other words, beds out and uses colour on a colossal and prodigal scale.' The examples that were drawn on – bluebell woods, hillsides covered with heather, masses of furze and broom – were precisely the examples used by William Robinson and others to argue for massed planting in the wild garden, and its striking effect can be seen in both these watercolours. The ideal was

broadness of effect, not variety: great sheets of daffodils or other bulbs naturalized in grass, or plants like oxalis and comfrey that would spread of their own accord. As S.W. Fitzherbert put it in his *Book of the Wild Garden*: 'Far better too few genera, species and varieties than too many. On Alpine slopes and South African veldt Nature scatters her flowers in wide drifts of one species and this should be our guide in the wild garden.'

THE BLUEBELL WOOD
Beatrice Parsons

THE RHODODENDRON DELL, KEW GARDENS
Ebenezer Wake Cook

The earliest, and most important, attempt by the Victorians to introduce a brighter range of colour into the landscape was the use of rhododendrons. Its remarkable success can be seen in the profusion of colour in the picture by Rowe. *Rhododendron ponticum* was being grown as an ornamental pot plant by the beginning of the nineteenth century; by the 1840s gardeners were discovering that it had the capacity to seed itself, and were beginning to fill their woodlands with it. The red-flowered *R. arboreum* from the Himalayas first bloomed at The Grange, Northington, in 1825, and hybrid forms were soon being raised, most notably at Highclere, Hampshire, after which 'Alteclerense', the most important of the early hybrids, was named. The spectacle of the Highclere rhododendrons reminded one writer in the 1830s of Claude Lorrain's sunsets, and after the introduction of a wide range of Himalayan species by Joseph Hooker from his expedition to Sikkim in 1847–51, the colour range was greatly enlarged.

Shown here is part of the magnificent rhododendron collection at Kew. It was first planted in the 1850s with Joseph Hooker's introduc-tions, and was rearranged by him in the 1880s as a series of concentric circles. Ebenezer Wake Cook (1843–1926) was born in Maldon, Essex, and quickly became a competent landscape artist. He studied in Paris and for a time worked under M. Chevalier. His work became much sought-after during his lifetime and he exhibited regularly at the Royal Academy and the Royal Institute of Painters in Watercolour. Although he did many of his best-known works abroad, mainly in Switzerland and Italy, his English ones, especially the garden scenes of this type, are particularly beautiful.

THE GARDEN PATH
Ernest Arthur Rowe

PENJERRICK, FALMOUTH
Beatrice Parsons

CHERRY BLOSSOM
Beatrice Parsons

From the 1850s onwards the number of new hybrid rhododendrons became ever greater. A swathe of nurseries such as Standish and Noble, Waterer's, and Veitch's flourished in Berkshire and Surrey, energetically producing new varieties. As the idea of the wild garden grew in the 1880s, many landowners began to experiment themselves with hybridizing in their woodlands; by the Edwardian period, gardens like Leonardslee in Sussex and Bodnant in Wales were becoming known for their hybrid collections, even before the flood of Chinese species collected by men like George Forrest and Kingdon Ward began to arrive in Great Britain.

In Cornwall and the south-west, the new hybrid rhododendrons fitted easily into the great, existing subtropical gardens, laid out on picturesque principles in imitation of wild nature. Some of the most famous hybrids were raised at Penjerrick, shown here.

The debates over massing versus variety that attended the wild garden made themselves felt in the rock garden as well. William Robinson encouraged the use of broad masses of alpines, a tendency that Reginald Farrer was to caricature as 'better a hundred yards of Arabis than half a dozen vernal Gentians'. Farrer attacked the massing approach in his preface to E.A. Bowles's *My Garden in Spring* (1914): 'But "garden" why call it? There are no plants; there is nothing but colour, laid on as callously in slabs as if from the paint-box of a child.' The rockery in the picture above, with its clumps of primulas, aubrietas and narcissus, is an example of massing on a small scale.

CHERRY BLOSSOM
Beatrice Parsons

The most popular form of wild gardening was the naturalizing of bulbs in grass, a technique which, since Robinson had urged the planting of bulbs under trees, could be carried out with a greater degree of formality than his other proposals. Daffodils, tulips, bluebells (all used as underplanting in the scene on the left), anemones, snowdrops, violets, crocuses were among the plants Robinson recommended.

Along with such planting went an increased interest in the use of flowering trees – often entailing an emphatic rejection of the exotic conifers so enthusiastically taken up at mid-century. Once again, the great question of colour planning arose. Robinson recommended planting in masses for broad effect: 'It is generally not easy to use these flowering trees in the flower garden, when that is very near the house, except in an orchard... They, or the hardiest of them, should be massed or grouped where they will come into the picture – whether seen from the house or otherwise... An excellent point in favour of Thorns, Crabs, Almonds, and Bird Cherries is that, in their maturity, they, in groups or single specimens, stand free on the turf – free, too, from all care; and it is easy to see how important this is for all who care for English tree-fringed lawns – a long way more beautiful than any other kind of tree garden.' On first coming to England from Ireland, Robinson had been employed in the herbaceous department of the Royal Botanic Society's garden in the inner circle of Regent's Park (since replanned as Queen Mary's Garden); scenes such as this, with mature trees growing freely, surrounded by well kempt grass falling away to the lake, although set in the Park proper outside the boundaries of that garden, would have been familiar to him.

REGENT'S PARK
Beatrice Parsons

LILY POND
Beatrice Parsons

Late Victorian literature contains more advice on the planting of bogs and of watersides than on the treatment of aquatic plants themselves. Moist soils, unsuitable for formal gardening. lent themselves nicely to the wild garden, and plants like gunnera and irises gave colour and beauty of form to the stream bank (the yucca and agapanthus shown in the picture on the right arc quite startling for a water-garden scene). It was not until the 1890s that a major fashion began for aquatic planting – and that hardy hybrid waterlilies, the work, first of the French nurseryman Latour-Marliac, and then of James Hudson of Gunnersbury House, were developed.

S.W. Fitzherbert, in his *Book of the Wild Garden*, urged for the water as well as the wild garden the importance of broad effects and a restraint upon variety; Nature 'is content to limit her materials'. 'One often sees little ponds and circular, artificial basins, in which several varieties of hardy Water Lilies are growing that crowd each other and hide the water... When the added beauty of water is vouchsafed to the pleasure grounds it is of the first importance that it should remain a clear mirror, reflecting the varied forms of trees ... but if water vegetation is allowed to spread and cover the pond these felicitous incidents can no more be witnessed.' The illustration above conforms to his principles, while he would have condemned the watercolour on the right for its overcrowding.

WATER GARDEN
Beatrice Parsons

A PAUSE FOR REFLECTION
Caroline Paterson

The idea of the wild garden grew largely out of the practice of embellishing woodlands. We have already remarked on the increasing use of rhododendrons and other flowering shrubs for this purpose. From the beginning of the 1860s, the nurseryman Peter Barr was offering seed packets of mixed annuals for scattering along woodland walks and waste places; bluebells, primulas, and spring bulbs were being used by the 1860s at gardens like Cliveden, Berkshire, for planting the more remote and less formal regions of the estate. The little girl in Caroline Paterson's picture is surrounded by a characteristic mixture of the favourite plants used for this purpose.

The concept of the wild garden as expounded by Robinson was based on the naturalization of exotic plants, but he devoted a chapter of his book *The Wild Garden* to native English flowers, and as the century wore on, more and more use was being made of native wild flowers in wild gardens. Foxgloves, daffodils, tansy, cornflowers, celandines, and the like were finding a greater place in gardens by the 1880s; the architect John D. Sedding, in his *Garden-Craft Old and New* (1891), wrote: 'I would devote a certain part of even a small garden to Nature's own wild self, and the loveliness of weed-life.' Some city parks, such as those of Hull, created wild flower displays; emphasis on wild flowers could have an educational effect at a time when the increasing rarity of several species was becoming noticed.

A SUMMER'S WALK
Helen Allingham

SPRING
Beatrice Parsons

Beatrice Parsons, perhaps the supreme artist of the wild garden – as these evocative pictures show – was born in Peckham, south London, in 1870, one of twelve children of Arthur Parsons, a translator at Lloyd's. She trained at the Royal Academy Schools where she learned to draw and paint in the manner of the Pre-Raphaelite followers; she won a number of prizes and exhibited from 1888 at the Royal Academy, at first showing large canvases of religious subjects. It was her brother-in-law Robert Emerson Dowson who later brought her garden watercolours to the attention of Dowdeswell's, and it was here that she held her first 'one-man' exhibition in 1904, where 40 out of 44 pictures were sold.

In 1907 she moved from Hampstead to Oxhey in Hertfordshire, where she lived with one of her sisters and remained for the rest of her life. It was a good place to work; many of the large houses near her, such as Oxhey Grange and J. Pierpont Morgan's estate at Well Hall, had well-known gardens and supplied her with excellent material. She worked not only in England but also in Italy, France, and Algeria. In 1911 E.T. Cook, then editor of *The Garden*, published *Gardens of England* with her illustrations; her pictures were reproduced in other gardening books, and it is easy to see why Sutton's chose to reproduce her extremely attractive watercolours on the covers of their seed catalogues for several years during the 1920s.

THE LAST DAYS OF SPRING
Beatrice Parsons

THE COTTAGE GARDEN AT HADDON HALL, DERBYSHIRE
Ernest Arthur Rowe

CHAPTER V

THE REVIVALIST GARDEN

T H E typical country house garden of the High Victorian period had made an open prospect an essential feature. But during the 1860s and 1870s an alternative trend in garden design had slowly developed, which placed its emphasis on seclusion and enclosure. The designers of such gardens looked back to the sixteenth and seventeenth centuries for their models; the result was usually called the 'old-fashioned garden', the 'old-world garden', or 'the pleasance'. The great precedent for such gardens was Arley Hall in Cheshire, created in the 1840s and much admired by late nineteenth-century architects; its features, walls, yew hedges, and herbaceous borders, became the stock-in-trade of the old-fashioned garden.

From the 1880s the old-fashioned garden spread widely in popularity, thanks largely to the propagandizing efforts of the Hon. Eleanor Vere Boyle, who wrote under the pseudonym of E.V.B. Her book *Days and Hours in a Garden* (1882), first published as a series of articles in the *Gardeners' Chronicle*, became a major literary souce for garden making in the next generation. At her estate, Huntercombe Manor, Buckinghamshire, beginning in 1871, she divided the garden into corridors and enclosures by means of yew hedges, and turned a section of it into a 'wilderness' on an eighteenth-century model. A decade later, the young architect Reginald Blomfield furthered the cause by his book *The Formal Garden in England*, in which he denounced the Victorian fashion for exotics and urged a return, not only to sixteenth- and seventeenth-century design features, but to more traditional forms of planting – fruit trees in an orchard instead of conifers in a pleasure ground. Such books helped to popularize an atmosphere of nostalgia for a garden world of quiet serenity – a world far removed from the colourful display of the High Victorian country house garden.

Surviving seventeenth- and early eighteenth-century gardens – not to mention some nineteenth-century restorations which were successfully passed off as the real thing – became a favoured subject for painters such as George Samuel Elgood and Ernest Arthur Rowe. Elgood, indeed, painted some pictures of Victorian gardens which gave them a spurious antiquity by portraying figures in the costume of the previous century. These paintings found a ready market, and helped to promote the cause of the old-fashioned garden.

Not all approved of this new trend in gardening; the writer William Robinson denounced these paintings for promoting a false ideal of the garden: 'We have seen in Bond-street a variety of picture exhibitions devoted to gardens, generally of the trifling stippled water-colour order. The painters of these pictures, for the most part-ten-minute sketches, have one main idea – that the only garden worth picturing is the shorn one, and pictures of such places are repeated time after time; a clipped line of Arbor-vitae, with a stuffed peacock stuck by the side of it is considered good enough for a garden picture. Work of this kind, which is almost mechanical, is so much easier than the drawing of a garden with the elements of varied beauty in it.' It is true to say that in such paintings it is the structure of the garden, not ornamental planting, that is important. Blomfield placed much emphasis in his book on period garden buildings and ornaments, but here the painters were ahead of him; sundials, dovecots, decorated gateways, old walls and hedges, had themselves become respectable subjects for painting by the 1890s.

A further subject, destined to prove much more controversial, was gradually becoming apparent in contemporary gardens. Topiary had been the most reviled aspect of Renaissance gardening, and its revival in the nineteenth century had been slow and uncertain; but after 1850, architectural topiary (imitating walls, columns and the like) had become suddenly acceptable. Sculptural topiary, however, was still proscribed by the dominant taste, and only slowly in the 1870s and 1880s did figures, such as birds and crowns, become more popular. In 1890 the architect John D. Sedding's posthumous book *Garden-Craft Old and New* threw down the gauntlet: 'in the formal part of my garden my

COUNTRY GARDEN
Lilian Stannard

yews should take the shape of pyramids or peacocks or cocked hats or ramping lions in Lincoln-green, or any other conceit I had a mind to'. And, despite the furious attacks of William Robinson for the next forty years, sculptural topiary became a popular fixture of the garden, as nurseries grew up which made the sale of ready-made topiary figures a speciality.

By the end of the century, the garden of hedged or walled enclosures, with topiary and Renaissance-style sculptural ornaments, and largely hardy planting, whether herbaceous borders or orchards, had become a settled vernacular for garden design. More readily adapted for the small middle-class garden than the display styles of the High Victorian period, and popular with architects because its formality gave them a greater role in the creation of the garden, it became the basis of the 'arts and crafts' gardens of the Edwardian period, and thus remained a significant influence on the twentieth century. Hidcote, which was begun in 1907, has been claimed as the most influential garden of the present century; but its series of hedged garden rooms and variety of topiary specimens was not an innovation, but the inheritance of a quarter-century of historical revivalism in the late Victorian garden.

IN THE GARDENS, LEVENS
Walter Tyndale

Levens Hall in Westmorland was by the end of the nineteenth century one of the most famous specimens of garden antiquities in England, frequently painted, and praised for its 'old-world' character. It is ironic to note to what extent it is a nineteenth-century restoration. The garden was planned at the end of the seventeenth century by Guillaume Beaumont, but fell into neglect in the late eighteenth, and was restored by the new head gardener Alexander Forbes after 1810. There is no evidence that topiary had existed in the garden before his time; the yews may well have been simply parterre bushes that had grown out of control. If in clipping them into shape he was restoring genuinely old topiary there is no evidence to show whether the resulting patterns were the former ones or his own invention. The box edgings and the figures in golden yew at least are definitely his. As early as the late 1830s, however, the topiary, with its emblematic figures of judge's wig, crowned lion, and the like, was being regarded as genuinely ancient, and as topiary became popular in the second half of the century, so the fame of Levens grew, and artists like Elgood and Tyndale made the journey to Westmorland to paint the gardens.

Walter Tyndale (1856–1943) was born in Bruges and came to England at the age of sixteen. He first painted in oil, until he moved to Haslemere where he met and was influenced by Helen Allingham. He travelled abroad in Europe, the Middle East, and the Far East and, despite the charm of pictures such as this one, among his best-known watercolours are a series published as *Japanese Gardens* in 1912.

LEVENS
George Samuel Elgood

THE BOWLING GREEN, BERKELEY CASTLE
George Samuel Elgood

'Uncertain tradition', reported a writer in William Robinson's magazine *The Garden* in 1900, 'says that the monks of Worcester cut and trained the avenue', which would suggest that the yews were around four hundred years old even then; more recent estimates, however, date them to the late seventeenth century. The sixteen yews were proclaimed 'a masterpiece of garden handicraft' by Gertrude Jekyll, and were said to represent the twelve Apostles and the four Evangelists. (Such designations for yew topiary were not uncommon in the nineteenth century; the yews at Heslington Hall were known as the Twelve Apostles by the

1830s, at least, and the yews planted at Packwood in the 1850s – already passing as Cromwellian in date by the end of the century – were supposed to represent the multitude at the Sermon on the Mount.) 'Such gardens as that at Cleeve Prior', continued the *Garden* journalist, invoking the legend of monkish antiquity, 'could not have been unknown to Shakespeare, and we may certainly conceive that he was thinking of [them] when he conjured up his visions of quaint garden beauty.'

At Berkeley Castle, Gloucestershire, the small formal garden illustrated by Kip in the early eighteenth century had disappeared by

the 1880s, when Lady Georgina Fitzhardinge began a restoration programme. The bowling green, however, or at least some of the hedges around it, were agreed by Elgood's contemporaries to date from Tudor times. Elgood on more than one occasion used costume figures, as here, to suggest the antiquity of the gardens he depicted – thus giving a spurious antiquity even to nineteenth-century gardens. Both topiary gardens have been ornamented with typical late nineteenth-century 'old-fashioned' flower borders, featuring plants like sunflowers, introduced in Tudor times, and red-hot pokers, an eighteenth-century introduction.

CLEEVE PRIOR
George Samuel Elgood

THE TRYSTING PLACE
George Samuel Elgood

The garden at St Catherine's Court, Somerset, was greatly enlarged and planted in the Victorian period, first in the 1840s by Colonel Strutt, then by Mrs Drummond. By the turn of the century, however, these additions, notwithstanding Mrs Drummond's bowling green, were dismissed as inferior by commentators such as Inigo Triggs; it was instead the early seventeenth-century structure of steps and terraces which attracted praise. Architects were turning away from the recreated formal gardens of the High Victorian period, looking instead for surviving examples of Tudor and Stuart stonework to provide more historically authentic models. The topiary and herbaceous planting shown in Hunn's painting were nineteenth-century embellishments.

The figurehead of this movement was Reginald Blomfield, whose *Formal Garden in England* (1892) catalogued the architectural remains of Renaissance and Baroque gardens. 'Since the disappearance of the formal garden', he wrote (provoking William Robinson's complaint that the major Victorian gardens had been formal), 'the necessity of scholarly design for garden buildings has been forgotten, and the result is seen in buildings and details, which are not simple and childlike, but wholly pretentious and bad.' The masonry of the eighteenth century, he thought, was 'probably the best that ever was done in England', and he particularly praised designs such as the one illustrated – gate piers with moulded tops and bases supporting round ornaments such as cannonballs or urns. He recommended planting 'gardens of roses and lilies, or of poppies' to accompany such architectural features, and 'to contrast with the horrors of a nursery gardener's catalogue'.

ST CATHERINE'S COURT
Thomas Hunn

THE APOLLO, BALCASKIE
George Samuel Elgood

AMORINI, MELBOURNE
George Samuel Elgood

The great Victorians had looked back to Tudor and Jacobean gardens with as much fondness as their Edwardian successors, but Blomfield and his contemporaries extended their taste a generation further on. The French style of the early eighteenth century was attracting favourable notice, and the principal surviving examples, Bramham Park and Melbourne, were both painted by Elgood. At Melbourne, Derbyshire, from about 1704, George London and Henry Wise had created a yew-hedged parterre and a formal woodland, sub divided by allées radiating from rond-points, and decorated with fountains and lead figures such as these by Van Nost. Gertrude Jekyll called Melbourne 'a precious relic of the past', and condemned mid-Victorian alterations for 'the ill effects of the modern planting of various conifers'. 'The tall trees inclosed by massive yew hedges, the pools and fountains, the statues and other sculptured ornaments, all recall, with their special character of garden treatment, the times and incidents that Watteau loved to paint.'

Balcaskie, Fife, in Scotland, was altered by William Sawrey Gilpin about 1850, but still preserved many aspects of its seventeenth-century design, including such statues as the Apollo shown here, standing serenely against a dramatic backdrop of foliage.

HAMPTON COURT
Cyril Ward

THE PRIORY GARDEN, HAMPTON COURT
Cyril Ward

In the heyday of the landscape garden, Hampton Court was scorned as an example of the formal taste ascendant in the age of William III; by the early nineteenth century, this formality was being praised once again, and throughout the Victorian period it was the most publicly accessible example of a garden which retained seventeenth-century features. Nonetheless, from the 1840s to the First World War, annual displays of bedding and then of carpet-bedding proved highly popular with the crowds that frequented the gardens, and from the 1880s it became one of the first public gardens to promote the cause of the herbaceous border. But, by the Edwardian period, a taste for authentic restoration was emerging; the flower beds were grassed over during the First World War because of the labour shortage, and it was proposed not to reinstate them, but instead to return the garden to its early eighteenth-century condition.

Cyril Ward (1863–1935) was born in Oakamoor, Staffordshire. He was educated at Denstone College and later went to Selwyn College, Cambridge. He returned to his old school to teach from 1885 to 1888. His natural leanings, however, were towards art, and he left Denstone College in 1888 to become a professional artist. Ward concentrated on painting landscapes and garden scenes. He used a subtle technique and was an accomplished draughtsman. In 1912 he published a book entitled *Royal Gardens*, combining his own faithful and detailed illustrations with descriptions of the gardens by their head gardeners and his own notes on garden design.

WALMER CASTLE
Lilian Stannard

These two gardens are both nineteenth-century versions of antique gardens. Walmer Castle, Kent, was the official residence of the Lord Warden of the Cinque Ports. The gardens were begun at the beginning of the nineteenth century, during William Pitt's time as Lord Warden, by his niece Lady Hester Stanhope. The first Duke of Wellington had the moat turned into a kitchen garden, but the major work was carried out under Earl Granville, who commissioned William Masters to turn the moat into a flower garden and create a terraced garden with a broad walk, shown here. At the time this picture was painted the Marchioness of Salisbury was directing the planting of the flower borders. 'The arrangement of the walk is entirely her conception'.

wrote Norman Brown in the *Gardeners' Chronicle* for 1898, 'and she prefers, as is seen, the old or variegated style of growing in preference to that adopted by many of the horticultural experts of the present day – the growing in masses of the same plant.' The high walls and arbours subdividing the gardens created an air of antiquity to which late Victorian visitors readily responded.

The garden at Penshurst Place, Kent, originally dates from 1570–1666, and was depicted by Kip at the beginning of the eighteenth century. Beginning from about 1850, the vernacular revival architect, George Devey, took Kip's view as his model for restoring the gardens, recreating the parterre and the walled enclosures. Reginald Blomfield held up Devey's

work as a model for garden architects to follow, and in his *Formal Garden in England* (1892) he particularly praised the prominence of fruit trees within the formal garden, as depicted in Ernest Rowe's picture: 'Nothing can be more beautiful than some of the walks under the apple-trees in the gardens at Penshurst. Yet the landscape gardener would shudder at the idea of planting a grove or hedge of apple-trees in his garden. Instead of this he will give you a conifer or a monkey-puzzle. . . Again, the pear-tree and the chequer-tree, the quince, the medlar, and the mulberry are surely entitled by their beauty to a place in the garden. It is only since nature has been taken in hand by the landscapist and taught her proper position that these have been excluded.'

THE SUNDIAL, PENSHURST
Ernest Arthur Rowe

BLICKLING
Beatrice Parsons

JULY
Charles Earle

The 1860s saw the advent of a new fashion in architecture: the imitation of seventeenth-century houses, using red brick, with much attention to gables, tile-hung roofs, and ornamental chimney stacks. This movement was quickly, and rather inaccurately, named 'Queen Anne' architecture, and it was accompanied by a distinctive movement in garden revivalism, based on the walled or enclosed garden. Andrew Murray complained in the 1860s that High Victorian fashion was based too much on the open prospect, and had no room for the sense of enclosure: 'Another consequence ... is the doing away with the walls of the garden. Having destroyed the garden, why retain the walls? ... it has certainly come to this – that in new places the garden walls are dispensed with, and the garden itself is represented by the shrubbery in front... There is a sense of snugness and security in a walled garden which is not found in any shrubbery. however much closed in.'

Blickling, a Jacobean House, shown on the left, illustrates the type of building admired by the new generation, and was a pioneer in the 1870s in replacing bedding by herbaceous plants in its parterres. The watercolour above illustrates the fashion that grew up from the 1870s of clothing a building in vegetation – most frequently ivy, although clematis, Virginia creeper, and as in this case, wisteria, were frequently used. The artist, Charles Earle (1832–93), was mainly a landscape painter who worked in England and in Europe and who would occasionally turn his hand to scenes such as this. He exhibited at the Royal Academy from 1857, and was elected a member of the Royal Institute of Painters in Watercolour in 1882.

GREAT TANGLEY MANOR, SURREY
Ernest Arthur Rowe

The revival of the walled garden brought with it a form of horticultural revivalism in the determination not only to base the design of the garden on historical precedent, but to limit the choice of plants according to period precedent as well. Books such as John Parkinson's *Paradisus Terrestris* (1629) provided lists of flowers grown in seventeenth-century gardens, and these became the staple of the 'old-fashioned' gardens that accompanied the new 'Queen Anne' houses of the 1860s and 1870s – actually based on seventeenth-century Anglo-Dutch style houses. Mrs Loftie. cousin of the 'Queen Anne' architect J.J. Stevenson, greeted the revival ecstatically: 'We rejoice heartily, so far as the science of gardening is concerned, at the new turn of the wheel which has given us back those dear old flowers. Queen Anne has come into her own again, and the train of faithful and enthusiastic subjects with whom she has returned bring in their hands proud turncap lilies and stately hollyhocks to plant against a background of moulded brick or stately yew . . .'. Despite this, note the presence of an abutilon, not exactly an old-fashioned flower, among the phlox and Michaelmas daisies in Beatrice Parsons's picture.

Great Tangley Manor was acquired by Wickham Flower in the 1880s and restored with the aid of the architect Philip Webb. The moat was cleared and returned to use, yews were planted, and a series of timber screens was erected to frame a formal garden. The only portion of the derelict garden that was preserved was the orchard, where many of the fruit trees were still surviving.

October, Abbotswood, Buxted
Beatrice Parsons

A SUMMER'S EVENING
Thomas Lloyd

The attempt to return to an English vernacular in the last quarter of the nineteenth century led architects away from Stuart Anglo-Dutch houses to half-timbered Tudor ones like Rumwood Court as models for their buildings, and led gardeners to try to rediscover the horticulture of the English past. A cluster of English vernacular names – larkspur, candytuft, meadowsweet, thrift, rocket – reappeared in garden writing, partially ousting the botanical Latin in which the previous generation had

carefully trained itself. William Robinson published a treatise on clematis, *The Virgin's Bower*, which freely invented vernacular names like 'alpine virgin's bower' for each species; he also popularized the 'authentically English' name 'rockfoil' for saxifrage, despite the fact that the name 'saxifrage' dates back to the fifteenth century.

Thomas James Lloyd (1849–1910), or Tom Lloyd as he is more commonly known, showed artistic talent from an early age, and began

exhibiting regularly at the Royal Academy and the Royal Society of British Artists early on in life. He lived in London, later moving to Sussex where he painted a large number of coastal scenes. He was a successful artist during his lifetime, and his pictures are instantly recognizable by his fluid and spontaneous use of watercolour. Here the tranquil garden scene is enlivened by the darting, swooping swallows, untroubled by the watching cat and the young girl reading to her grandmother.

RUMWOOD COURT, LANGLEY, MAIDSTONE
Helen Allingham

PEACOCK IN A GARDEN
George Samuel Elgood

PEACOCK BY A SUNDIAL
George Samuel Elgood

George Samuel Elgood (1815–1943) was one of the finest painters of garden water-colours, as the pictures shown here and elsewhere in the book amply illustrate. He was fascinated by formal gardens and spent numerous hours painting them. The basic background for many of his watercolours was the interesting shape of sculpted hedges silhouetted against the sky, their range of subtle greens offset by a profusion of different colours in the flower border; he avoided scenes with full sunlight because light reflected from leaves tends to weaken the colour effect of flowers. Elgood exhibited over 100 pictures at the Royal Institute of Painters in Watercolour,

and held over a dozen one-man shows at the Fine Art Society in New Bond Street from 1891 to 1923. It was probably Elgood's work that inspired Robinson's diatribe quoted at the beginning of this chapter.

In 1904 reproductions of his pictures appeared in *Some English Gardens*, with text by Gertrude Jekyll; he then went on to illustrate special editions of two of the Poet Laureate Alfred Austin's popular gardening narratives, *The Garden that I Love* and *Lamia's Winter Quarters*, as well as contributing pictures to *The Studio's* three volumes on *The Gardens of England*. A critic wrote about Elgood in *The Studio* in April 1904: 'To paint flowers – simply

– or in gardens – demands of the artist something other than a technique which subordinates everything to the vulgarity of its own self-assertion; it demands tenderness, lightness and patience, as from petal to petal the artist advances with what in a lifetime he has gathered of skill. Mr. Elgood's gardens satisfy all these requirements.'

Peacocks frequently appear in the pictures of Elgood and his rivals. The garden writer E. V. B. (Eleanor Vere Boyle) entitled one of her books of essays *The Peacock's Pleasaunce*, and discussed the symbolic meanings of the peacock in traditional lore, which made it a suitable denizen of the old-fashioned garden.

PEACOCKS IN A GARDEN
Ernest Arthur Rowe

Ernest Arthur Rowe (1863–1922) was Elgood's principal rival as a garden watercolourist and, like him, exhibited regularly at the Royal Institute. He lived for a time in London but spent most of his life in Tunbridge Wells where he could readily find delightful subject matter such as this local garden. Such was his popularity that between 1899 and 1913 he held eight one-man shows at the Dowdeswell Galleries in London.

Rowe was one of the most competent of the late Victorian watercolourists. He specialized in painting formal gardens, and in many of his finest watercolours, every flower is carefully delineated. A critic in the *Connoisseur*, reviewing his one-man show in 1921, commented that, 'His drawings of old-world gardens are always pleasing... Dealing in detail rather than with broad effects, he sometimes permits himself to be carried away by a comprehensive observation of minutiae, with the result that a few of his more laboured studies lack reticence and become spotty in construction and coloration.'

In the picture above the two peacocks draw the eye past the brightly-coloured mixed borders and through the handsome gateway to the parkland beyond.

RUSTHALL, TUNBRIDGE WELLS
Ernest Arthur Rowe

THE ABBEY GARDEN
Albert Goodwin

SUNDIAL
Alfred Parsons

Alfred Parsons (1847–1920) started life as a Post Office clerk. He later studied at South Kensington, where he became Professor of Art. He was elected ARA and RA in 1897 and 1911 respectively, and became President of the Royal Watercolour Society in 1913. As a botanical artist he is best known for his drawings for Ellen Willmott's *Genus Rosa* (1913), although he was contemptuous of the lithographic reproduction in that work; he also illustrated the later editions of William Robinson's *Wild Garden*. In the 1880s he became part of the artists' colony at Broadway, Worcestershire, and played a part in designing gardens in the Midlands and West Country, most notably Wightwick House and Mary Navarro's garden in Broadway. The picture shown here mingles the revivalist theme of the sundial with the emphasis on flowering trees – including the not exactly old fashioned rhododendrons – which Parsons was helping to promote by his association with Robinson.

Albert Goodwin (1845–1932) was an admirer of Turner whose influence manifests itself in many of his watercolours. In his 'Abbey Garden' he manages to convey that moment when evening light and the smoke from a bonfire fuse to give an ethereal feeling to the subject. The delicate colours and careful stippling technique make this a particularly fine example of the artist's work.

He was born in Maidstone, Kent, and was a pupil of the Pre-Raphaelite associates Ford Madox Brown and Arthur Hughes. In 1872 he went to Italy with John Ruskin and Arthur Severn; he also travelled widely in India and Egypt. He was elected a member of the Royal Watercolour Society in 1881 and held a number of one-man shows, including one at Birmingham City Art Gallery. He spent most of his life at Arundel, and his *Diary* (1883–1927) was published in 1934.

THE SUNDIAL
Thomas Mackay

Ernest Albert Chadwick was born on 29 February 1876 at Marston Green in Warwickshire, the son of the draughtsman and wood engraver, John William Chadwick. He showed an early aptitude for drawing and later studied art at Birmingham and at Hampton. This watercolour is typically well observed and the garden scene shows his usual excellent sense of colour.

Images like these are typical of the 'old-fashioned' or 'old-world' garden as interpreted by fashionable painters around the turn of the century. Its primary characteristics are enclosure, a design that is formal without being geometrically complex, a strong architectural element, and a certain range of garden ornaments as accessories: fountains, lead figures, and above all sundials. 'Sundials', wrote Reginald Blomfield, 'have always held an honoured place in the formal garden, sometimes on the terrace, sometimes as the centre of some little garden of lilies and sweet flowers. Everyone loves them because they suggest the human interest of the garden, the long continuity of tradition which has gone before, and will outlive us.' The opening years of the twentieth century saw the production of books devoted purely to sundials and their mottoes; as Blomfield's statement implies, they were the perfect ornament for gardens that strove to convey an 'old-world' flavour, to suggest a link with tradition without being slavishly tied to a well-defined period.

SUNDIAL
Ernest Albert Chadwick

CHAPTER VI

INTO THE TWENTIETH CENTURY

'In a sense we are all gardeners to-day', wrote Walter P. Wright in his book *The Perfect Garden* in 1911. 'Cultured people talk of gardening as they talk of books, and paintings, and music . . . A knowledge of gardening is a part of education.'

The important role accorded to gardening in Edwardian life was the result of many forces working in the late nineteenth century, not least of them the increasing emphasis on the smaller, middle-class garden, where the owner of the house took the responsibility (or at least the credit), instead of the country house garden which was in a sense a separate institution from the house, managed by a professional staff. But the role of the painter was also important in helping to fix the image of the sort of garden that was desirable.

Of the painters included in this anthology, the only one to make explicit statements about garden design was Cyril Ward, whose watercolours of Hampton Court are reproduced on pp. 134–5. In his book *Royal Gardens* (1912), he gave his support to the architectural fashions of the day by demanding that every garden ought to be laid out with a definite plan, but he placed no importance on historical accuracy in design. For his analysis of the desirable aspects of a garden, he turned not to architects but to a painter, the Slade Professor C.J. Holmes, who had recently published *Notes on the Science of Picture-Making*. Holmes named unity, vitality, infinity, and repose as the four essential qualities of a good painting; these Ward reinterpreted in garden terms. Unity meant the organization of the garden around a principal centre (or centres) of interest; vitality, 'bold arrangements of light and shade, and . . . schemes of contrasting colour'; infinity, the concealment of views so as to suggest something beyond; and repose, the simplification of ornament. These qualities can certainly be found in the paintings of old and old-fashioned gardens made by Ward, Rowe, and Elgood, as well as in the less historically minded work of Beatrice Parsons, Lilian Stannard, and the like; and they can be seen as well in many of the

THE LITTLE FOUNTAIN, DRAKELOWE
Beatrice Parsons

gardens that were made or became popular in the Edwardian period. The well-framed garden scene, enclosed rather than looking out on an open prospect, with a simple formal design and brightly-coloured borders, was the legacy of these painters to twentieth-century gardening.

As representative examples of such Edwardian gardens, let us take three: Drakelowe in Derbyshire, The Hill, Hampstead, and Sutton Place in Surrey. Drakelowe, the garden of Sir Robert Gresley, was known as a 'Dutch' garden of the period of William III; in 1906 Reginald Blomfield restored the house, and designed a garden temple; a new balustraded terrace with turf walks was laid out by his collaborator Inigo Thomas. The result was featured in *Country Life*, where Avray Tipping described it as 'altogether charming and satisfactory', praising 'that characteristic sense of enclosure which is essential in a good garden'. It was also featured in E.T. Cook's *Gardens of England*, with one of Beatrice Parson's watercolours (of the new rose garden). The Parsons shown here depicts a different area, lauded by Tipping for the 'admirable effect of hedges and turf'.

The Hill, Hampstead, was a garden designed by Thomas Mawson, later first President of the Institute of Landscape Architects. It was the London house of Lord Leverhulme, for whom Mawson had designed gardens elsewhere in the country, and contributed to the creation of the model industrial city Port Sunlight. The site was chosen for its panoramic views of London and the ground level was raised with infill from the excavation of Hampstead underground station; work began in 1904, and the garden was extended in 1911. It was laid out as a pair of descending terraces, each enclosed by pergolas 'in the Italian style' – columns of Portland stone with beams of English oak. All the architectural features were softened by planting; semi-circular holes were cut in the stone paths to allow climbing plants – jasmines, wisteria, clematis, the newly popular rose 'Dorothy Perkins' – to grow up over the pergolas.

Sutton Place was a sixteenth-century house; Sir Richard Weston obtained title to the property in 1521. In the Edwardian period it was the property of Lord Northcliffe, and Lady Northcliffe was busy overseeing the redevelopment of the garden. Horace J. Wright described the finished work in the *Gardeners' Chronicle* for 1911: 'Sutton Place has no garden of set geometrical design ... flower-beds with regulation bedding find no place; on the contrary, it is a garden of clever unconventionality in which the visitor finds surprises at every turn.' (For many people, the abandonment of the bedding tradition still had the force of novelty). New features included rose, water, and rock gardens, and an extensive wild garden traversed by neatly mown paths.

The most famous feature of Sutton Place was its collection of herbaceous borders, described by Charles H. Curtis in the *Gardeners' Magazine* of 1911: 'A very fine feature of the older part of the garden is the arrangement of flower borders. These are everywhere. They intersect the fruit and kitchen garden squares, and extend along under the outer walls ... In most cases the planting is in groups, and each group may consist of two or three subjects, that will follow each other in the floral calendar, and yet not interfere with each other's development.' One border was devoted to Darwin and May-flowering tulips, a second to herbaceous peonies and daffodils, a third to pink aquilegias and Darwin tulips, a fourth to perennial asters, a fifth to delphiniums and Canterbury bells, a sixth to irises; the seventh was the 'blue border', with delphiniums and *Anchusa italica*. The border illustrated, called 'Lady Weston's Walk' after the sixteenth-century family, and also referred to at the time as the 'Tudor border', shows the continuing fascination with old-fashioned plants. Curtis held up these borders as models to follow: 'close planting is the order, and [they provide] a fine object-lesson in the art of producing a continuous display without recourse to big stocks of reserve plants.'

In all three of these gardens we can see the qualities Cyril Ward had claimed as essential: enclosure, formality, simplicity, and colour. But the progression from Drakelowe, through The Hill, with its architectural elements swathed in vegetation, to Sutton Place with its close-planted borders, also illustrates a growing tendency: the union of the 'old-fashioned' garden, with its formal outline and sense of enclosure, and the 'cottage garden' with its rich and indiscriminate mixture of plants. This combination was to become one of the staples of twentieth-century garden design in England. Take, as a celebrated instance, Lawrence Johnston's garden at Hidcote. In design, it was an impressive example of the late Victorian tradition of the 'old fashioned' garden: a series of chambers and walkways, enclosed by walls and hedges, each planted in a different style. But now read Vita Sackville-West's description of the planting: 'Would it be misleading to call Hidcote a

THE HILL, HAMPSTEAD
Ernest Arthur Rowe

cottage garden on a most glorified scale? It resembles a cottage garden or rather a series of cottage gardens in so far as the plants grow in a jumble, flowering shrubs mingling with roses, herbaceous plants with bulbous subjects, climbers scrambling over hedges, seedlings coming up wherever they have chosen to plant themselves. Now in a real cottage garden, where limitations and very often the pattern – for example the curve or straightness of a path leading from the entrance gate to the front door – are automatically imposed upon the gardener; the charming effect is ... very largely accidental. But in a big garden like Hidcote, great skill is required to secure not only the success of the planting, but the proportions which can best give the effect of enclosure ...' Here the revivalist garden of hedged enclosures and the myth of the cottage garden have been neatly dovetailed together.

This, then, is the legacy bequeathed to our century by these late Victorian garden painters – they have left us not merely a depiction of a fascinating period in garden history, but an image that has helped to direct the course of gardening into our own times.

LADY WESTON'S WALK, SUTTON PLACE,
Thomas Hunn

FURTHER READING

Pictures by artists included in this book may be seen in the following:

AUSTIN, ALFRED, *The Garden that I Love*, 1906 ed., (Elgood); *Lamia's Winter Quarters*, 1907 ed., (Elgood)

BRADLEY, A. G., *Worcestershire*, 1909, (Tyndale)

CALTHROP, DION CLAYTON, *The Charm of English Gardens*, 1911, (Barton, Elgood, Beatrice Parsons)

COOK, E. T., *Gardens of England*, 1908, (Beatrice Parsons)

ELGOOD, G. S., *Italian Gardens*, 1907; *Some English Gardens*, with text by Gertrude Jekyll, 1907 and later eds

FREEMAN-MITFORD, ALGERNON, *The Bamboo Garden*, 1896, (Alfred Parsons)

HOLME, C. G., ed., *The Gardens of England in the Southern and Western Counties*, 1907, (Elgood, Rowe); *The Gardens of England in the Midland and Eastern Counties*, 1908, (Elgood, Rowe)

HUISH, MARCUS B., *The Happy England of Helen Allingham*, 1903

HYATT, ALFRED, *A Book of Old-world Gardens*, 1911, (Beatrice Parsons)

MAETERLINK, MAURICE, *Old-fashioned Flowers*, 1906, (Elgood)

MESSEL, LUDWIG, *A Nymans Flora*, 1918, (Alfred Parsons)

PATERSON, ARTHUR, *The Homes of Tennyson*, 1905, (Allingham)

ROBINSON, WILLIAM, *The Wild Garden*, 1881 and later eds, (Alfred Parsons)

SIEVEKING, A. FORBES, *The Praise of Gardens*, 1899, (Elgood, Walker)

Suttons' Seed Catalogues 1920–25, (Beatrice Parsons)

THOMAS, H. H., *The Ideal Garden*, 1910, (Beatrice Parsons, Rowe); *Practical Amateur Gardening*, 1920, (Beatrice Parsons frontispiece)

VON WYSS, C., *Gardens in their Seasons*, 1912, (Elgood, Beatrice Parsons)

WARD, CYRIL, *Royal Gardens*, 1912, (Ward)

Ward Lock's All about Gardening, 1927, (Beatrice Parsons, Elgood)

WILLMOTT, ELLEN, *The Genus Rosa*, 1914, (Alfred Parsons)

WRIGHT, HORACE J. & WALTER P., *Beautiful Flowers and How to Grow Them*, 1922, (Beatrice Parsons frontispiece)

WRIGHT, WALTER P., *The New Gardening*, 1912, (Rowe frontispiece); *The Perfect Garden*, 1908, (Lilian Stannard frontispiece); *Popular Garden Flowers*, 1911, (Lilian Stannard); *Roses and Rose Gardens*, 1911, (Beatrice Parsons)

INDEX

Page numbers in *italics* refer to illustrations

ILLUSTRATION ACKNOWLEDGEMENTS

The illustrations in this book have been reproduced by kind permission of the following:

CHRIS BEETLES LTD, ST. JAMES'S, LONDON pp. title, 46, 51, 62, 86,
87, 90, 91, 95, 97, 101, 109, 111, 115, 116, 117, 120, 121, 126, 128, 130, 132, 133, 134, 135, 139, 140,
141, 143, 145, 147, 148, 149, 155, 156

FINE-LINES FINE ART pp. 10, 26, 30, 31, 42, 48, 59, 63, 64, 68, 74, 83,
89, 92, 94, 96, 112, 127, 129, 151

DAVID JAMES pp. 28, 29, 35, 36

SHEILA HINDE FINE ART p. 72

KENULF GALLERY pp. 54, 66, 122

THOMPSON'S GALLERY pp. 98, 108, 125, 131

PRIORY GALLERY pp. contents, 18, 21, 24, 25, 27, 32, 33, 37, 38, 47,
50, 52, 53, 55, 56, 58, 60, 65, 67, 70, 71, 73, 84, 136, 138, 142, 150

PHILLIPS pp. 16, 85, 88, 113, 118, 153

PRIVATE COLLECTION pp. half-title, 34, 81, 82, 100, 114, 144

RICHARD HAGEN LTD pp. 41, 69, 80, 99, 106, 110, 137

SPINK & SON LTD p. 146

BRITISH MUSEUM pp. 39, 79

THE LEGER GALLERIES LTD pp. back cover, 119

MR & MRS HAROLD DEVINE front cover

CHRISTOPHER WOOD GALLERY p. 107

RICHARD GREEN GALLERY p. 12

BOURNE GALLERY pp. 8, 102

SOTHEBY'S pp. 20, 22, 40, 49, 57, 61, 93

ABBEY ANTIQUES & ARTS p. 19

CHRISTIE'S p. 23

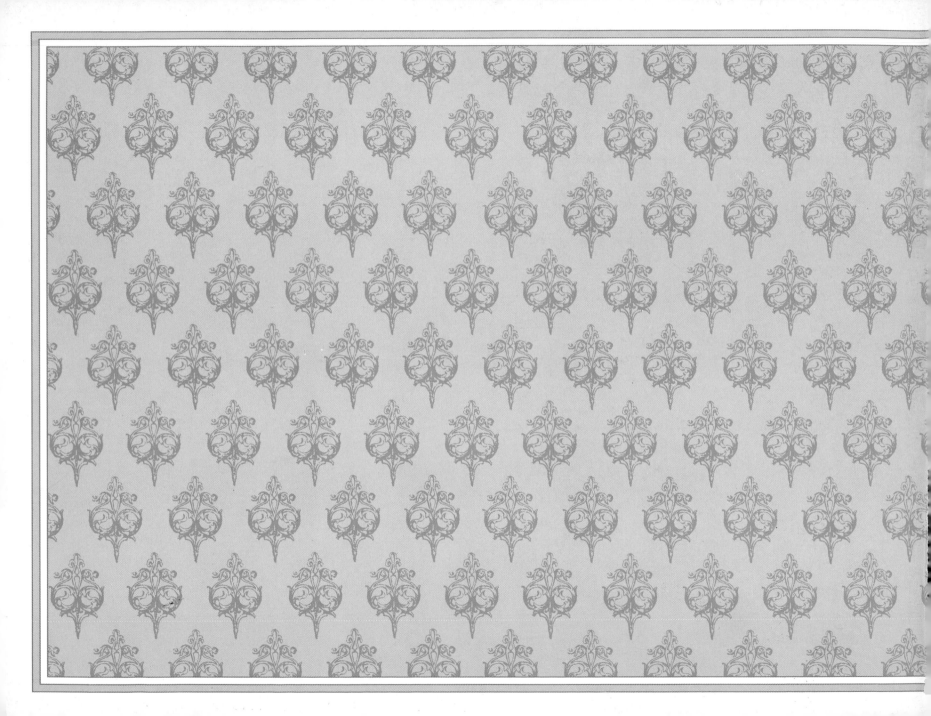